Detour
To Financial Freedom

Live, Save, Retire and Enjoy

LUDY BALDOZA CABANAS

Archway Publishing books may be ordered through booksellers or by contacting:

Archway Publishing
1663 Liberty Drive
Bloomington, IN 47403
www.archwaypublishing.com
844-669-3957

ISBN: 978-1-6657-2785-3 (sc)
ISBN: 978-1-6657-2784-6 (hc)
ISBN: 978-1-6657-2786-0 (e)

Library of Congress Control Number: 2022914121

Print information available on the last page.

Archway Publishing rev. date: 02/13/2023

Dedication

To My Grandchildren:
      Anais Lourdes Cabanas
      Felix Monk Werden
      Raphael Paul Cabanas
      Uma Sparrow Werden

Contents

Acknowledgments

Zarah Cabanas for suggesting this project and to all her assistance in making this a reality

Tony Cabanas for being my sounding board and tough critic

Reme-Antonia Grefalda for being there in my struggles in the beginning and for her continued support

Paz R. Nolasco, Esq. who in spite of a very tight schedule as she was flying home to the Philippines, was able to find time to write the Foreword.

The various lectures, webinars and online training from Author Learning Center, Jerry Jenkins, Steve Harrison, Paper Raven Books, and Alison Wearing, among others.

Greg Castilla as an inspiration

Diwata Midel Cahapay and Cynthia Brawner, my high school classmates, who both listened to my complaints

Henjie Jensen, Concierge Archway Publishing from Simon and Schuster, who was so patient with and understanding of me, and always soft spoken and well mannered.

Foreword

Detour to Financial Freedom Live, Save, Retire and Enjoy is an interesting book for legal immigrants like me specifically the chapter on starting from scratch. Like Ludy Cabanas, the author, I migrated to America with just my law degree and experience. I worked with a publishing company dealing with taxes for thirty years.

Ludy Cabanas, is a determined person. Reading the book leads the reader to that conclusion. I met Ludy through her husband Antonio. He and I worked together as lawyers of a financial company in Makati, Philippines.

Detour to Financial Freedom deals with her struggles to financial freedom and a happy and stable retirement. The book definitely helps the reader overcome similar struggles the author went through. She and Antonio worked hard to meet their goals of a comfortable retirement, travels, and fun. Ludy was epitome of determination in achieving their goals. She left a comfortable life in the Philippines to spearhead their plan to achieve those goals. She met obstacles along the way but her determination didn't deter her from achieving their goals. She overcame immigration problems, acquired legal status, and was able to bring the family to the United States of America.

The chapter on credit cards and debts is enlightening. It outlines the author's road to meet her and Antonio's goals through the use of credit cards to meet their daily needs, Sallie Mae for the education of their kids, and other loans. It lists the pitfalls of using revolving credit, and the strategy to a debt free lifestyle.

Detour to Financial Freedom also has some historical insights that make a reader relate to the author's stories. It also shares her experiences during her travels. Over all the book is a very good read.

PAZ R. NOLASCO, Esq. Vigan, Ilocos Sur, Philippines

Chapter 1

My Retirement Predicament

We had just seven years before full retirement. Was it possible to retire with only $32,445.19 saved in my individual retirement account (IRA)? That amount did not even make a dent in our current debts to my creditors.

During all my productive years, I had worked so hard to eliminate debts and achieve financial freedom. But I was wallowing deep in debt. I couldn't sleep without thinking about why I was in this situation. What had brought me to this horrible financial crisis? How was I going to get out of this hole and achieve my retirement dreams? The money owed to credit card companies and other creditors amounted to more than triple my annual salary. All my dreams were fading away quickly.

I had been married for thirty-two years to Tony, who is fourteen months older than me. He and I had acquired as many credit cards as we could under my name or in his name. Some had been issued to me with him as the extended user; others had been issued to him with me as the extended user. Further, we'd transferred balances from one credit card company to another with offers of an increased line of credit, a lower interest rate and a longer period of due date. This process allowed us to accumulate more in credit card debt. We were good credit cardholders as we were never late in our payments. However, we were capable of paying only the minimum due, and thus, we accumulated an incredible amount of debt with compounding interest.

In addition to our credit card debt, also outstanding was the Sallie Mae account for our daughter's student loan. This was a good debt. Never had we regretted signing up for this loan. She deserved to study at New York University for a bachelor of fine arts in film and television.

We were living paycheck to paycheck. Basic living expenses were not even covered by our net monthly income. My thinking then was why worry about retirement savings when we were not even sure if we would have enough to live on? Was retirement really attainable under these circumstances? How and why would we even think of retirement?

In 1987, American Express was the first company to grant me a credit card with a revolving credit line of $500. As an immigrant with a credit card, I felt empowered to become part of mainstream America. A credit card revolving line was like a security blanket or a buffer in the event I was laid off. Unemployment benefits were not sufficient to support a family. Before my brief period of unemployment in 1992, I had already secured five credit cards with a total reserved credit line of $100,000. During this unemployment, how could I possibly put food on our table, pay the rent for our two-bedroom apartment, pay for gas and maintenance on my Toyota Celica, pay the monthly premium for health insurance for my family, or pay my children's school expenses and other living costs? It should be noted that in 1991, Tony was struggling to find employment as he has just joined us in the United States.

According to an article by Thomas A. Durkin as published in the Federal Reserve Bulletin in September 2000, three surveys were conducted in 1970, 1977 and 2000 by the Survey Research Center of the University of Michigan and sponsored by the Credit Research Center. Overall opinion about credit cards was somewhat more negative and polarized in 2000 than it had been a generation ago, especially among holders of bank cards. Opinions among all families that credit card use was "good" registered a bit higher in 2000 (33 percent) than in 1970 (28 percent) but a bit lower than in 1977 (39 percent). The view that card use was "bad" was stronger in 2000 than in either of the earlier years. Durkin mentioned that credit cards originated in the 1950s as a convenient way for the relatively well-to-do to settle restaurant and department store purchases without carrying cash. They also serve as a payment device in lieu of cash or checks for millions of routine purchases and for many transactions that would otherwise be inconvenient or impossible to conduct.

Credit cards have also become the primary source of unsecured open-end revolving credit, largely replacing the installment-purchase plans previously used in retail businesses ("Credit Cards: Use and Consumer Attitudes, 1970–2000," https://www.federalreserve.gov/pubs/bulletin/2000/0900lead.pdf).

Regardless of the results of these statistics and surveys, I was thankful that we had available credit cards to use for all our needs and wants.

Soon I had regular employment, and fortunately, the company provided health insurance for its employees. It is not mandated for companies to provide health care for their employees. Small businesses can hardly afford to offer this benefit to their employees. An immigrant who was just establishing himself or herself in the US workforce did not have much choice but to accept any employment that was first offered. I did not have many options to seek employment in companies offering the best benefits or terms. I had to take what was available or face the alternative—a possibility of longer unemployment.

I had the potential of landing good employment. But with limited local experience, it would take some time for that potential to kick in. With no one and nothing to bank on but my own limited resources, I worked doubly hard to make ends meet and be self-sufficient.

I aspired for a life that had meaning and quality. I wanted not just to survive but to thrive. The trouble, however, was that I was used to a certain kind of lifestyle, and it was hard to make a downward change. One good thing was certain: alternative resources of credit were readily available to provide those needs and the lifestyle. I took full advantage of it. Further, I opted to take a calculated risk of living the life I wanted for myself and for my family, hoping to make the necessary adjustment as time allowed.

Chapter 2
Credit Cards and Debts All Over

Our income, like that of average working people, was not enough to cover even the basic requirements of living. Obviously, Tony and I considered saving for retirement a low priority. At the time, our main concern was funding our daily needs. We were in debt, and we could not fathom how we could pay for them. If we did get out of debt, how long could we continue to be debt-free? Would there be a retirement to secure our future? When the time came, would we still have full physical and mental capacities to face accumulating money for retirement? How many of us are in this situation?

Per Statista.com, and published by Raynor de Best on November 25, 2020, the value of revolving credit in the United States between 1995 and 2019 was held mostly in consumer credit cards, meaning no fixed number of payments in contrast to installment credit. The amounts held were as follows (I only selected five-year increments):

1995	-	$408 billion	
2000	-	$645 billion	increase of 58.1 percent
2005	-	$815 billion	increase of 26.4 percent
2010	-	$876 billion	increase of 07.5 percent
2015	-	$900 billion	increase of 02.7 percent
2019	-	$001.07 trillion	increase of 18.9 percent

From 1995 to 2019, there was an increase in the value of revolving credit by 162.2 percent. In this time frame of twenty-five years, consumers' usage of credit card ballooned by $662 billion. People were funding their consumer needs by credit. We were part of these statistics. We were chasing the American dream and living life in mounting debt ("Value of Revolving Credit Outstanding in the U.S. 2020," October 4, 2021, https://www.statista.com/statistics/214277/total-revolving-credit-outstanding-in-the-united-states/).

How many credit cards do you carry? According to *CNN Money*, published in March 2013, three percent of Americans have no credit cards, 44 percent have one or two, 37 percent carry three to five, and 16 percent have more than five credit cards. Overall, Americans have an average of four credit cards. Credit card optimizers might be curious if there were such a thing as having too many credit cards. There really was no one-size-fits-all answer ("Poll: How Many Credit Cards Do You Carry?" *CNNMoney*, https://money.cnn.com/POLLSERVER/questions/64055.fullpage.question.html).

In the same report, the average credit card interest rate was 14.58 percent ("Credit Card Interest Rates for December 13, 2012, Yahoo, December 13, 2012, https://finance.yahoo.com/news/credit-card-interest-rates-dec-080046381.html).

An average person in the United States had $6,194 in credit card debt as it appeared in the 2019 Experian Consumer Credit Review ("Average American Credit Card Debt by State—Alaska Tops the …" November 1, 2021, https://www.cnbc.com/select/average-credit-card-balance-by-state/). The average amount of credit card debt per household in the United States stood at $5,700 ("Chart: Credit Card Interest Rates Keep Climbing," *Statista*, August 13, 2019, https://www.statista.com/chart/19010/credit-card-interest-rate/), and each had an average credit limit of $22,751. It advised to be mindful of credit scores, finances, and personal goals. It all depends on how responsible you are at managing multiple credit cards. Pay on time and in full ("What Is an Average Credit Card Limit? *CNBC*," https://www.cnbc.com/select/average-credit-card-limit/).

Tony and I were a total exception to these statistics and information. We had twelve credit cards, and with those cards, we had accumulated a total debt of $324,328. Let me show you why we doubted we would be able to retire and enjoy a debt-free life.

Here was the breakdown of our debts that were listed in the uniform residential applications, settlement statements, and other statements:

Year	Debt Balance	Creditor	Number of Credit Cards	Average Balance per Credit Card
1998	$46,050	Various	7	$6,579
2001	$35,000	Honda for Odyssey van	0	$580 per month
2004	$102,317	Various	12	$8,526
2004	$47,000	Toyota for Lexus	0	$660 per month
2006	$87,982	Home equity line of credit (HELOC)	0	Variable
2006	$35,540	Various	4	$8,885
2006	$73,380	Sallie Mae	0	$416 per month
2008	$25,986	Various	3	$8,662
2009	$26,453	Various	7	$3,779
2010	$15,822	Home Depot	0	Pay in full in 18 months

These credit card debts, auto loans, student loan and home equity lines of credit (HELOCs) afforded us a fruitful, healthy and happy life. The Home Depot debt was interest-free for eighteen months. The auto loan from Toyota Motor was with an interest rate of 4.99 percent per annum. As mentioned previously, the Sallie Mae loan was for the education of our daughter at New York University from 1999 to 2003. She graduated with honors, which was more than enough to compensate for this cost. A good education presupposes a good future. HELOC was used to pay off credit cards. Our regular monthly income after deducting federal income tax, state income tax, Social Security tax, and Medicare tax was insufficient to cover our daily living costs. These credit card debts sustained our lives.

The debts above were not those of a typical American person or family. Had we overdone our approach to good living by relying on credit without the backing of good income and resources? Could we wind up wrinkled, sickly, old and still debt-ridden and dirt-poor in the twilight of our lives? I don't mind being old and wrinkled, but with good health and money sufficient to lead a grandiose life at the end of the day. Was it still doable? This scenario had put me and Tony in a reassessment mode. We considered our priorities and objectives at the end of our healthy productive days. There were times when I was at the point of despair. But I always believed that if there were problems, there must be solutions. But how do you find the solutions to these myriad cash-flow problems?

The above listed debts were paid from refinancing our residence, our first purchase. As shown in the chart, as of 2009, our credit card debts were paid from our salaries and the advance from HELOC. Non-credit card debts, like Home Depot, auto loan, and student loan, were outstanding. HELOC was being paid monthly with an interest rate of 3.75 percent, compared to credit cards' average interest rate of 14.99 percent.

To be debt-free was one of the goals, and to retire with a million dollar was the magic amount that Tony and I dreamed of. Strategies to achieve these objectives had to be learned and put in to practice. Changes in our lifestyle and priorities must be drawn and mapped out. And there was not much time to waste. It was critical for these changes be done now, otherwise we would be working until our dying days.

Chapter 3
American Dreams

1. Home Ownership in the United States

We lived in a garden apartment for nine years before we moved to our first home in the same neighborhood. Finding the right house for our two children, Carl and Zarah, was not easy. We wanted our house to be in the same school district and the same neighborhood they were used to. The Rock Creek Forest Subdivision was not cheap based on our incomes. Rosalie was an angel real estate agent and put forth an extraordinary effort to find us a suitable match and guided us to being able to afford the purchase.

In the Philippines, six months into our marriage, Tony and I moved to our first home. It was funded through the Social Security System (SSS), a state-run social insurance program for workers in the private, professional and informal sectors. SSS members can avail themselves of maternity, sickness, disability, retirement, funeral, and death benefits. SSS also allows qualified members to take salary, housing, business and educational loans ("Social Security System (Philippines), "SSS - Social Security System - Purpose, Functions, and Responsibilities ...." https:// owwamember.com/sss-social-security-system/. "Social Security System Philippines Benefits." 13 Sept. 2020, https://thephilippinestoday.com/ social-security-system-philippines-benefits/.

After contributing for seven years, we were able to borrow against my funds to finance the purchase of our home in the Philippines. SSS became the mortgagee. Just like in the United States, the SSS pension depends on your contribution and length of service. When I became self-employed, I stopped contributing to my SSS fund. I did not believe then that it was necessary. A member can collect a monthly pension if he or she has contributed at least for ten years. I was short of it. I rectified this on reaching my retirement age.

We sold the Philippine house and used some of the proceeds for the down payment for our first home purchase in the United States; the rest were used for living expenses. We have a trusted real estate agent-friend who took charge of the sale and proper remittance of the proceeds to us in the United States. We were totally happy with this experience.

We settled quite comfortably in our first house in the USA as recommended by Rosalie. It was perfect for us.

Our first home in the USA (First Purchase)

The subdivision had well-lit sidewalks on both sides of the road. The neighborhood was so clean, with well-trimmed lawns and shady trees. The neighbors were friendly and even held potluck parties during summer. The school district was one of the best in the county and state. The recreation center was located in the neighborhood park. There were tennis courts, basketball courts, soccer and football fields.

The walk/bike trail was close by. During three seasons of the year, this park was teeming with activities. It was a wonderful place to live.

Originally it had three bedrooms and two and a half baths. The lower level was renovated for a fourth bedroom with a full bathroom. An extra room was made that could be a den or an extra bedroom if needed. A good-sized pantry, an organized laundry room, and lots of storage spaces were built. A 20-foot × 20-foot composite deck was built, and the porch and walkway were replaced by brick with decorative design only after having lived there for twelve years. Every now and then, kitchen appliances and bathroom fixtures were replaced and repairs done to make the home a little cozier.

This first home brought us a lot of happy memories. My children brought their friends to the house. I loved to feed them Filipino dishes like chicken-pork adobo, and lumpia Shanghai (eggrolls). I also loved to make pansit, which is made of rice noodles, chicken or shrimp, snow peas, carrots and spring onions. I hosted several parties for charity organizations, and Bicol Choral Group entertained us and our guests with Christmas carols in English and Filipino. Thanksgiving, birthdays, and anniversaries were celebrated with families and friends in this home.

Special events also took place in this house. One was the engagement of our son, Carl to Laurence. Another was the visit of my son's would-be in-laws and family to share Christmas dinner with us and to get to know each other's families. Laurence's parents, including her grandmother, flew in from Paris, France. Her sister and family came from Germany, and her brother and family came from North Carolina.

We welcomed the first visit of our granddaughter on a Thanksgiving Day. Carl and his family live in Columbus, Ohio. There have also been many visits from our daughter, Zarah and Matt, who live in Brooklyn, New York and in a country home in Livingston Manor, New York.

We lived in this home for twenty years, and it has been filled with happy memories. We still have this lovely property but as a rental now.

2. Children's Schooling

Carl was the best student in summer camp at Maryland Science Center in grade school. For middle school, he qualified for both the Humanities and Communication Arts Magnet Program and the Science Magnet. He opted for the former, so he could improve his communication skills and speak better English since it is not our first language. For high school, he went to Blair Magnet School for Science, Mathematics, and Computer Science. He was one of the hundred, from more than eight hundred applicants, accepted from Montgomery County schools. He interned at the National Institutes of Health in Bethesda, Maryland, in radiology during his senior year. He was involved in sports, music, church, and the Boy Scouts. He achieved the Boy Scouts' highest rank, Eagle Scout.

Our main concern for our children was to send them to school and for them to earn a degree and be able to provide for themselves and their own families in the future. We were just ordinary employees making a decent living but not enough to cover all the needs and wants. For college, Carl wanted to pursue a course in medicine, radiology in particular. "For preparatory medicine, I'd like to enroll at a college in California," he told us. That's a three-hour time difference and five-hour flight, not counting any check-in and check-out times and any layover. A day is lost to traveling. In addition, it was a very expensive school. Maybe we could accommodate his needs when he told us, but during his pursuit of studies for medicine proper, we could "run out of gas," and it would be a disaster for him and us.

"Enroll at the University of Maryland, College Park for premed, and get a BS in biology. Then consider other schools for medicine proper in the future. It is what it is," I said. It was accepted and everyone was happy. He got into the honors program.

However, during his third year, he came to me and said, "Mom, I don't think I have the patience of a doctor. I'd like to go back to my original love of computer studies." I was relieved with what I heard. UMCP is one of the better schools offering courses in computer science and engineering. It meant he would stay in town, and the costs were within reasonable bounds.

But it wasn't just a matter of patience. Our son's grades were not very good. Why? "Mom, I did not know that I should keep my grades up to continue in the honors program," he explained. Carl secured a job in a computer engineering company while he was in his junior year. He was offered a promotion when he graduated, which he did in due time.

Zarah is three years and eight months younger than Carl. One day she asked me, "What is the similarity between a lake and a mountain?"

"Lake is water, and mountain, land," I replied. "I don't know. What is the similarity? They are both part of nature."

"They are both land forms," she answered. This was one of the questions asked in the oral examination when she was being considered for the Center for the Highly Gifted program in Montgomery County. Along with forty-nine other selected students, she attended the center. While divided into two groups, each fourth-grade class was comprised of students with fifth-, sixth-, seventh-, and even eight-grade levels in mathematics, reading and science. From ninth to twelfth grades, she qualified for and attended the Humanities and Communication Arts Program for middle school, just like her brother. She developed a great interest in writing, broadcasting, and alto sax. She switched from violin to saxophone, which she enjoyed and excelled in.

In high school, she became interested in communications media. She started the daily school video morning program, which she named Info Flow. She was a Girl Scout, a cantor in our church, played alto sax in the school's jazz band, served as producer of Info Flow, took private piano and saxophone lessons, and took tennis lessons at the Columbia Country Club. She participated in science competitions and won awards. For her achievements, she was recognized by the American Association of University Women (AAUW) in a ceremony at the Mansion in the Strathmore, in Bethesda, Maryland.

It was not hard to decide to invest in her education. For college, she wanted to go to University of Southern California (USC) or New York University (NYU) to pursue a career in film and television. She was adamant about going to California or New York. "California is out of the question. Make sure that you get admitted to NYU," I said. She succeeded in getting an early admission to NYU by December.

Once you let pass an opportunity, it is gone. The same thing with time. They never come back. As for money, you can source it, and that's all. We signed up for educational loans. Our children's educations were our main projects. There was no question about it. She helped out in her junior year as a resident assistant (RA). In exchange, she received room and board. She had undergone extensive interviews and training to handle situations that might come up in a diverse university community. As an RA, she developed leadership skills, compassion, and trained to solve problems.

Her undergraduate school movie project was presented at the main festival screening in the First Run Film Festival in 2003 at the Lincoln Center. Her film, *City Poems: Rio de Janeiro and Tokyo* was a semi-finalist for a Wasserman award. She was so relentless in her pursuit of excellence that she traveled to Rio de Janeiro, Brazil, to gather some inspirational materials for this project and to Tokyo, Japan, for the other part, thus the title. Zarah graduated with honors and earned a gold tassel on her cap. She completed internships at Nippon Hoso Kyokai (Japan Broadcasting Corporation, NHK), an international broadcasting company, and with an editing company called Red Car New York Inc. However, right after graduation, she was hired as a manager at *Whitehouse Post* in New York City. She tried many other fields along the line of her course of bachelor of fine arts in film and television.

Chapter 4
Social Lifestyle: The Price of ...

How did I get us into this debt trouble? I live my life, and in so doing, I take risks. I believe that if lack of money is the problem, it is easy to solve—just find it. If the problem involves health or a relationship, it is far more challenging to overcome. To have good health and happiness is of utmost importance. In order to achieve this goal, it is better to maintain good relationships and live a satisfied life. When I am healthy and satisfied, I'm happy. When I am happy, I extend that happiness and goodness to others. This is how I approach life, and that is what life means to me. We are quite lucky to be healthy and have good relationships, even if we have debts.

But this way of thinking brought us into deep financial trouble. Even without the income to sustain it, we resorted to funding our travels and purchases to conform to our lifestyle through credit card debts and money borrowed from other sources.

One day as I parked my car, I ran into my employer Abdi Parvizian, who was parking his Jaguar. "Ludy, why you're still driving that van? Your kids have long gone from home. Why don't you buy a car that's appropriate with your position?"

"Well, if you give me a raise, I certainly would love to," I replied.

I checked online and compared reviews and prices. And with Tony's help, we decided to test drive two or three car models and makes. One late afternoon, on our way to a birthday celebration for Bogie, son of our dear friends Ellie and Nick Cabanayan, we passed the car dealership and checked on a car. It felt good to be behind the wheel. We left the dealership driving a brand-new black Lexus 330 ES model 2004. We volunteered to drive the birthday boy to his own townhouse in our new car. Pointing at the beautiful sedan, this smart twenty-nine-year-old said, "Auntie, this is where your retirement fund goes."

We worked hard and were entitled to have fun, recreation and a good social life. We were in the social register of the Philippine Embassy. We were invited to some events and functions held at the embassy. One Philippine Embassy official had mentioned there were more than a hundred Philippine-American organizations in the metropolitan Washington DC area. For our pleasure and fun, we became part of a great social circle. We attended most of the gala and induction balls, fundraising activities, charitable auction events, beauty pageants, and just about any other event there was. There were professional organizations of medical doctors, lawyers, accountants, engineers, and associations based on the regions or places they were originally in the Philippines, like the Ilocanos of the north, the Bicolanos of southern Luzon, or Visayans or people of Mindanao regions. And alumni associations of schools, including Ateneo de Manila University, University of the East, University of the Philippines, Far Eastern University, De La Salle University, University of Santo Tomas, and the College of the Holy Spirit.

The annual Philippine independence celebration spread out during the month of June culminated with a gala dinner and dance. Officials of the Philippine embassy and consular office in Washington DC participated in this event. On this occasion, I invited my non-Filipino friends to attend and experience the culture showcasing Philippine traditional dances, music, some Philippine dishes, and to socialize with the Filipino community.

I was an executive officer, trustee, or board member of at least five organizations. For these many events that we attended in a year, how many gowns and evening wear did I purchase for these never-ending socials? How much did I pay for the tickets to attend each party? How about the donations and expenses, like the costs of hotels, restaurant meals, and so on. My son once dropped a comment about how popular we were.

Weekends were special, and how much more the long weekends! Day trips, overnight trips, visits to parks, shopping, dining out, movies, and many more ways to have fun with family. Shopping at upscale department stores for brand-name clothes, shoes and accessories were the norm. Not just for me but everyone in the family of course.

One of these escapades was an ocean cruise to Nassau in the Bahamas for three nights, plus a predeparture stay for three nights in Orlando (Port Canaveral), Florida. We went with friends in October 2002. On our drive heading down to Orlando, Tony and I took advantage of staying a day in a resort in Myrtle Beach, South Carolina, and another day in Savannah and Tybee Island in Georgia.

For the family's pleasure and to celebrate Tony's fifty-fifth birthday, we went to Puerto Rico for five days. The four of us stayed in a charming hotel in Old San Juan, and every day we had activities that were interesting to all of us. Puerto Rico had many similarities with the Philippines. The two countries were both Spanish colonies in the sixteenth century, and along with Cuba, both were ceded by Spain to the United States at the signing of the Treaty of Paris on December 10, 1898, which ended the Spanish-American War. Puerto Rico remained a US territory, and Cuba was granted independence. The United States paid twenty million US dollars to Spain for the Philippines. The Filipinos expected to be granted independence, just like Cuba, since they had revolted against Spain in 1896 long before the Americans got involved in the Spanish-American War of 1898. On June 12, 1898, the Philippines declared its independence from Spain ("Treaty of Paris (1898)," *Wikipedia*, https://en.wikipedia.org/wiki/Treaty_of_Paris_(1898).

The years 1898 to 1946 were an era of American colonization in the Philippines, which included the Spanish-American War and the

Philippine-American War from 1898 to 1902. It was the Philippines' fight for independence from the United States. In American history it was called the "Philippine insurrection" ("Milestones: 1899–1913—Office of the Historian," https://history.state.gov/milestones/1899-1913/war).

The Philippines gained its independence from the United States on July 4, 1946. Until 1962, the Philippines celebrated its Independence Day every Fourth of July, the same day as the United States celebrated its independence from England. However, in 1962, the Philippine government, under President Diosdado Macapagal, declared June 12 as Philippine Independence Day. Today, the Philippines celebrates July 4 as Philippine American Friendship Day.

In Puerto Rico, the El Morro and La Fortaleza were reminiscent of the Philippines' Old Manila and the Fort Santiago ruins. The colorful Spanish buildings, churches, thick walls surrounding the city, prisons and architecture were vestiges of Spanish colonialism.

Spanish structure in Puerto Rico

We enjoyed the visit to the tropical rain forest of El Yunque National Forest. A point of interest included the waterfalls, its whiteness contrasting with the green flora and canopy of trees. We had a good walk in this environment of greenery and rustling sound of the waterfalls.

One day, we boarded a boat to the island of Culebra and enjoyed Flamenco Beach. It had shallow turquoise waters and white sand. It stretched for a mile around a sheltered, horseshoe-shaped bay. To me, this is one of the most beautiful beaches, and in fact, it is the most beautiful beach in Puerto Rico. It is also consistently rank as one of the most beautiful beaches around the planet. Just around Old San Juan, there were also many nice beaches for people to enjoy. "Flamenco Beach - The Best & Most Beautiful Beach in Puerto Rico - 2022 ...." 09 Feb. 2022, https://www.puertoricotravelguide. com/flamenco-beach-puerto-rico/.

Many Puerto Rican dishes were made with plantain, yucca, rice, pork and chicken. Well-known favorites of the locals were mofongo, made from green plantains seasoned with garlic and salt and stuffed with chicken, beef, shrimp, or vegetables. Puerto Ricans have pernil; the Filipinos have the same but call it lechon. This was a whole roasted pig. Its skin was very crispy, and the meat so tender and flavorful. Especially when dipped in a sauce made of pureed liver with vinegar, pepper, salt, garlic, roasted onions and other spices.

Another family trip was to Niagara Falls, Ontario, Canada, for three days and two nights. We had time to bond as a family while enjoying these amazing waterfalls. We rode the Maid of the Mist boat. It gets you close to the enormous falls, where you can hear the thunderous sound of crashing water. We also enjoyed the journey behind the falls. An elevator took us thirteen stories below for a closer view of Horseshoe Falls.

How about a reward for deserving children? In 1996, Carl graduated from high school. What to do for summer? Boy Scout camping was done, and tennis, baseball, and track and field were interests of the past. He deserved a reward for graduating with good grades, earning the Eagle Scout rank, and being a good boy—no drugs, no smoking, no serious trouble. How about a European trip as a graduation gift? How about Zarah? She deserved a gift, too, since she had celebrated fifteenth birthday, and as siblings, it was better they have shared experiences. According to a friend who was a travel agent, Cosmos Travel had a great tour of six European countries for sixteen days.

At church, we had a friend whose daughter was a friend of Zarah. She was curious about my children's plans for that summer. Of course, what an exciting thing for Zarah to have a traveling buddy. Since she would have a girlfriend to travel with, shouldn't Carl have one too? I contacted a friend about her two sons, who were Carl's friends. One was already committed to go abroad with his friends from school, but one could go. The two boys and two girls were assigned an adult chaperone by the travel agency. They went to London, England; Paris, Nice, and Lyon in France; Brussels, Belgium; Lugano, Lake Lucerne, and Kuessnacht in Switzerland; Venice, Rome, Pisa, and Florence in Italy; and the principality of Monaco and Luxembourg. We provided Carl and Zarah with cash allowances and gave each of them a credit card. Yes, a credit card. Fortunately, both stayed within the generous budget, and the chaperone provided good feedback on this matter. Tony and I have not been to those places except that I had gone to Paris.

This was another instance of priorities. Most people might think that ours were misplaced. However, to our understanding of life, work must be balanced with reward and pleasure. We charged this expense to credit cards, resulting of course, to increased debts. And as for the retirement fund, it could wait.

Our children earned our trust through their responsible handling of the credit cards issued in their names. It resulted in developing their self-confidence and control. Their perspectives of the world broadened through travel and actual experiences. Alicia, Mike,

Zarah and Carl left for the tour happy, and they returned much happier, with stronger friendship ties, and richer in experiences.

The four high school tourists

The first thing they asked while still at the airport was for Japanese dinner. The three families had a great time listening to their children's stories over a spread of sushi rolls, sashimi, tempura, udon noodle soup and other Japanese favorites.

Our costly lifestyle could cause delay or even failure in achieving our retirement objective. It certainly meant continuing to live a debt-ridden life. Should we not worry about our mounting debt? But we thought we were great managers of our debt. We were never late in our payments. Of course, we paid only just a little above the minimum amount due. The horrible result was the monthly compounding of principal and interest. Not to worry. Maybe we could address that in due time. Meanwhile, we were going to live our lives. No need to worry now; there was still time. This was how I thought about retirement and debt issues. Can you believe it?

Chapter 5
Wrong Choices (But Rewarding Lessons)

In search of income and security, I joined a marketing organization engaged in retail networking of skin-care and nutrition products. I could get rich and become financially independent. At least that was the sales pitch. The people who introduced me to it were successful restaurant owners who lived in one of the most prestigious residential addresses in Maryland. In my mind, for them to already be wealthy but still engaged in this business meant there had to be something good in it. They wouldn't go into this venture unless it was worth their time, and there's money to be made from it.

However, to succeed in this business, you had to recruit members and make them recruit their members, and on and on. And, of course, sell products to them and their contacts. Money was made when you sold to your recruits and received commissions on their sales. The ideal way to make money in this system was to recruit at least three others. Each of these three should each recruit at least another three, who in turn, would do the same. On the third level, your group would have thirty-nine members, and on the fourth level, your team would have 120 associates. How many can you ideally recruit? You and all your recruits had to move the products to earn your commissions and overrides. In most instances, you end up buying the products and stock them. I saw it in my upline and her upline. That was my future too. I learned that this type of marketing comes and goes. The products selling hot now you probably won't see later.

I don't know how, but I got hooked again in networking. It

could be the prospect of lots of greenbacks that attracted me to it. This time it was in financial services. It was great! I studied and took and passed the license examination for life and health insurance. I did the same for securities so I could sell various insurance products and mutual funds (Series 6). I earned a license to supervise my financial associates (Series 26), the Uniform Securities Agent license (Series 63), and a license as an investment adviser (Series 65). These securities licenses are administered by the Financial Industry Regulatory Authority (FINRA) or by the North American Securities Administrators Association (NASAA). I also obtained a license in property and casualty insurance. In network marketing, one's success depends on the number of recruits and members on your team and the hierarchy you create. Build at least three strong legs, who should each have three legs as well. Just like the skin-care line, the more recruits you have, the more money you make. You sell the products to your recruits and recruits' recruits and your recruits' recruits' recruits while they are in training and with no licenses. Once they have licenses, they can do the same as they follow the same system. To be successful, you must be trainable, coachable and a good follower of the system. This is not a pyramid or Ponzi scheme. This is network marketing.

When you sell insurance products, you earn commissions. You also get override commissions on the sale of insurance and financial products of your recruit and recruit's recruits down the line. Percentages of commissions vary. Another way to earn your money is to write and close insurance accounts, variable annuities, or mutual funds on behalf of a trainee's recruits from another team. A trainee is not licensed, so he or she cannot write any policy or security product. You definitely deserve to share in the commissions from your downlines as you provide the training, office, maintenance and support.

I worked very hard with Tony always as my partner. I associated my group with the hierarchy of other senior uplines and established offices in McLean, Virginia; Skokie, Illinois; and in Rockville,

Maryland. My so-called run for the marketing director position was quite a challenge. Traveling to the offices in Maryland, Virginia, and Illinois was not easy. But I had to train my team members, close accounts, do business presentation meetings (BPM), and motivate the team to recruit and grow in number and knowledge. I taught them how to recruit, how to close accounts—that is, sell financial products—and, of course, to get licensed. When I was a recruit, I learned to be coachable and put the company business system into practice. "Company" here is not the insurance company but the marketing group. As required, I made a list of at least fifty people and more to be better. My list included family, friends, officemates, people in my church, neighbors, school, groceries, mail carrier and anybody I met. I learned how to start a conversation with a stranger by FORM: Ask them about *f*amily, *o*ccupation, *r*ecreation, *m*otivation. That was definitely effective for me.

During BPMs, commission checks were distributed. Team members were recognized for closing accounts, for passing insurance or securities licensing exams, for having recruits or new team members, and for being promoted from trainee to associate member to supervisor and to marketing director. Announcements of training classes, conventions and conferences were also made during the BPMs. The marketing director is a permanent position. At this level commissions earned are good enough to survive on. It was truly exciting to be called "marketing director," and I saw my checks coming in.

But then, somewhere along the way, I realized that was not for me. You put yourself under a lot of pressure to continue recruiting, building teams, and developing leaders to become marketing directors. In addition, you work for promotion to senior marketing director to chief executive officer. My passion for this kind of business fizzled. For several years I hung on, but I eventually had to let it go.

Though this was not for me, my experience in network marketing greatly improved my understanding of people and of life. In our trainings, we were encouraged to read books such as Stephen

Covey's *7 Habits of Highly Effective People*, Napoleon Hill's *Think and Grow Rich*, Robert Kiyosaki's *Rich Dad Poor Dad*, Thomas J. Stanley's *The Millionaire Mind* and *The Millionaire Next Door*, and Dale Carnegie's *How to Win Friends and Influence People*.

I met and strengthened friendships among my team members and associates in my hierarchy and other hierarchies. Did I make money? I did, but not like the ones who made hundreds of thousands and some lucky ones who made millions. The income I made barely covered my costs to operate, including attending conventions and producing promotional materials. I was partly successful, unlike some people who never attained the position of marketing director, never passed the licensure exams, never moved beyond trainee, and some who never made any money. I wondered if the incomes reported as earned by our leaders were sustainable in the years that followed. Had the income from commission income flattened out when accounts were terminated for nonpayment of premiums? Or on mutual funds and variable annuities when withdrawn by clients who sustained financial reversals, employment loss, or for whatever reasons?

The money I earned did not fully compensate for the time spent in this business venture. However, it was not a total loss. The knowledge and experience proved to be a bargain of a lifetime. How Money Works, Rule of 72, insurance and financial products were invaluable lessons learned in this chapter of my life. The Rule of 72 is a calculation that estimates the number of years it takes to double your money at a specified rate of return. This is based on the principle of compounding interest ("Rule of 72: What It Is and How to Use It," *Bankrate*, July 28, 2021, https://www.bankrate.com/investing/what-is-the-rule-of-72/).

For example, you are now thirty years old and plan to retire when you are sixty-six. You have $10,000 to invest. You put your $10,000 in an account that earns 2 percent interest. You take 72, divide it by 2, and the result is 36. That means your $10,000 will be $20,000 after thirty-six years. At age sixty-six, can you retire with

$20,000? If you are smarter, see what your investment of the same $10,000 in one that pays 4 percent interest. Take 72 divide it by 4, and the result is eighteen years. At age forty-eight, you have $20,000; at age sixty-six, you now have $40,000. Now check further. If you put it in an investment that pays you 8 percent, at the same age of thirty years and with the same $10,000, using the Rule of 72, your money doubles every nine years. At age thirty-nine, your money is now $20,000. At forty-eight, your money is now $40,000; at age fifty-seven, it will be $80,000. And at age sixty-six, you will have $160,000. How about if your investment earns 12 percent? Using the same formula of the Rule of 72, your money will double every six years. Let's see:

Age 30	-	$10,000
Age 36	-	$20,000
Age 42	-	$40,000
Age 48	-	$ 80,000
Age 54	-	$160,000
Age 60	-	$320,000
Age 66	-	$640,000

That is one reason why time and investment returns are critical in savings and investing. I take this Rule of 72 and apply it to the credit card balances that I owe. I check the interest rates. They range from 12 percent to 24 percent, with some as high as 29 percent. Do you wonder why credit card companies and banks are flourishing? I no longer wonder why my credit card balances add up every month even if I pay regularly. Because of the principle of compounding interest, you end up working just to pay for the interest on the debt. Without good financial information, I will never get out of the paycheck-to-paycheck mindset. This knowledge empowered me to recognize some common sense in my debt issues and earning capabilities.

Chapter 6

The First Glimpses of Europe and the United States

The first city I ever visited and fell in love with was Paris, France. It was in August 1984. I was a young Philippine attorney who joined the Philippine delegation to attend the International Law Association conference in France for a week. My travel was provided from my personal funds. I had a successful practice as a CPA-lawyer in metro Manila. Tony was a vice president of a financing company in Makati City. The Philippines was then under the regime of Ferdinand Marcos. It started when he placed the entirety of the Philippines under martial law by Proclamation No. 1081, dated September 21, 1972 (History of the Philippines: 1965–1986," *Wikipedia,* https://en.wikipedia.org/wiki/History_of_the_Philippines_(1965%E2%80%931986)).

Martial law was officially lifted on January 17, 1981. Marcos retained essentially all his powers until he was ousted and exiled on February 25, 1986.

We were not to speak ill about the president, the corruption, the violation of human rights, or anything derogatory about the Philippines. In short, we should lie. The conference delegation included the supreme court chief justice, associate justices, famous legal practitioners, judges, law professors, new lawyers like me, and many other legal dignitaries. At the plenary session on the first day, the Philippine supreme court chief justice was one of the speakers. He presented the Philippines and its government under President

Marcos in the best light, including its adherence to the rule of law and the respect for human rights, though it was under martial law. This was totally unacceptable to me. I was an idealist, a young attorney then. The delegates in our group were mostly government officials on a junket.

I decided not to attend any more of the conference sessions. And that was the start of a wonderful adventure. One day after finishing the tour of the Chateau de Malmaison ahead of the group, I invited some Filipino non-lawyers to enjoy some freshly baked pastries at a nearby café, including, of course, the baguettes with butter and marmalade. When we finished, the bus that was just across the street waiting for the rest of the group left without us. We had to find our way back to the hotel. I considered this the most fun part of the Paris trip. In 1984, English was hardly spoken in France. It was a problem because I didn't know any French. It took a while, but we eventually found someone who spoke English. He was a young man on his way to work at a bank in Paris. He was kind enough to lead us to the station and showed us how to use the Metro. At every stop, we went out and explored the place. One of the nice places we discovered in our own tour was Place de la Concorde. It is a vast public square, considered the largest in Paris. At the center of it is the Luxor Obelisk, an Egyptian artifact seventy-five feet high ("Luxor Obelisks," *Wikipedia*, https://en.wikipedia.org/wiki/Luxor_Obelisks).

We then continued our search for the Sofitel Hotel. At one stop, while still on the escalator, there it was, right in front of us. We had a great time exploring the City of Lights, we viewed the Mona Lisa at the Louvre Museum, went up to second level of the Eiffel Tower, saw the Arc de Triomphe by Champs Elysees, passed by the Moulin Rouge, explored Montmartre, sat on the steps of Sacre-Coeur Church, lazed in front of Napoleon Bonaparte Les Invalides and many more.

For the Philippine delegation and all attendees of the

International Law Association Conference, the Paris City mayor hosted a luncheon on the grounds of the city hall. The Philippine ambassador to France hosted a dinner for the Philippine delegation. There I saw the affluence of most of the people I was with. The children of some government judicial officials were studying at universities in Europe. I wondered how they could afford it.

Next on the itinerary was Vienna, Austria, where some of the Philippine delegation attended the International Convention of the American Bar Association, of which I was a member. We went to visit a nurse in Vienna, who is a niece of attorney Sedfrey A. Ordonez. She served as our tour guide in Vienna. We had delicious Filipino home-cooked meals at her flat.

After the European sojourn, I went to New York City, another very exciting place that I love. I stayed for a couple of days with our friend, a lawyer who was then a legal editor for a big publishing house. Thereafter, I proceeded to Washington, DC, where I visited Eve, my younger sister. She gave birth to her one and only child, Morgan.

I continued to bond with my conference co-attendee, Sedfrey A. Ordonez, my remedial law professor, who was visiting his brother and sister-in law, who were both medical doctors. He later became the solicitor general, secretary of justice, permanent representative of the Philippines to the United Nations and chairman of the Commission on Human Rights of the Philippines during President Corazon Aquino's presidency. He later had the opportunity to help shape a part of my career had I chosen to follow a particular path. Aquino won over Marcos in a snap election in February 1986. The People's Power Revolution toppled the dictatorship regime of Marcos, who escaped to Hawaii.

I went to Los Angeles, California, and visited a Filipino couple, clients who were exploring investment opportunities in there, as well as a prospective client in the travel agency business. From there, I went to Chippewa Falls, Wisconsin, and visited the Moats, the family whom my brother Vic lived with when he was an American Field Service scholar.

My trip back to Washington from Chippewa Falls was another first. I boarded a Greyhound bus for a twenty-three-hour bus ride, the longest I ever experienced. Among the stops we made were Madison, Wisconsin; Chicago, Illinois; Toledo, Ohio; Cleveland, Ohio, and Pittsburgh, Pennsylvania. This was my first time in this part of the United States. I wondered where the road was for the buses going in the opposite direction. In the Philippines, I saw buses on the same road going in opposite directions. But on this route, I didn't even see the road for vehicles going in the opposite direction. The roads were wide, and there were trees and greenery on the side of the road. This happened thirty-seven years ago, and it could be a different highway and much shorter travel time now.

Chapter 7
The Travel Bug Bites Hard

It was not until twenty-one years later that the travel bug bit again. I still remember how fascinating Europe was—its architectural designs of buildings and churches, parks, promenades, food and culture. The organized land tour from Trafalgar Tours dubbed as European Spotlight was for fifteen days and included London, England; Paris and Nice, France; Geneva, Switzerland, passing by Beaune; Monte Carlo, Monaco; Montecatini, Pisa, Florence, Venice and Rome in Italy.

There are many ways to visit places. For those who are employed and have limited vacation days, joining an organized package tour is the least cumbersome, and at the same time, you can cover many points of interest. The costs of joining optional tours are not included in the package and could be substantial but worth it. An unforgettable optional tour offered in Paris was a cabaret and dinner with champagne and unlimited wine at Le Moulin Rouge.

Paris Le Moulin Rouge cabaret and dinner

Preferred seats were reserved, and there was no waiting in line to get our tickets. We enjoyed an evening of exciting acts, stunning tableaux, and wonderful entertainment of the famous cancan. Had we not been with the group, we would not have done it. The group consisted of twenty couples and three solo travelers from Australia, New Zealand, Canada, South Africa, and the United States.

In Geneva, everyone opted to take the cruise on Lake Geneva (Lac Leman) aboard a steamer. We visited the most picturesque Savoyard lakeside medieval village of Yvoire, in France. Along the lake are palatial mansions of the rich and famous. It is known for its winding, hilly streets, with the old, stone houses of fishermen lined along them. Yvoire has quaint restaurants, just like in postcards, with flowers everywhere. The village is like a garden itself. The only trouble were the restrooms; there were not many of them to serve curious people like us.

Yvoire, France, garden-like village

We went back to Switzerland by motor coach, passing by the rich green fields of Savoy. Leaving Geneva again for the French Alps, we ascended Saleve mountain's 3,609-feet elevation by cable car in about five minutes. The views were exquisite from atop Mount Saleve. You can see Lake Geneva; Jet d'Eau, the large water fountain; the highest mountain peak of Mont Blanc and other mountains in the Alps; and the beautiful city of Geneva and its vicinity. We had a delightful dinner of French regional cuisine at a Savoyarde restaurant, perched on the limestone ridge that afforded the views below and the French Alps around.

From Geneva, we continued to the French Riviera and Nice. The beach that we went to does not have sand but pebbles—polished, large, flat, gray stones called "galets." They contribute to making the sea in Nice vibrant blue. Cannes, glamorous as it sounds, has sandy beaches, palace hotels, and the Film Festival Center. There was nothing really special in this place except the Cannes Film Festival Center, where international films are previewed annually and where film stars and other celebrities pirouetted in the latest fashion and style.

Another optional tour that we joined in the French Riviera was the drive along the Three Corniches, or the Cliff Roads. These dizzying roads were carved on the mountainside. The first is Basse Corniche, which runs parallel along the coast. In the middle is Moyenne Corniche, and at the top is the Grande Corniche, which is about 1,804 feet above sea level. The views were spectacular along perhaps the most beautiful coast in Europe. We passed expensive homes and villas with swimming pools overlooking the Mediterranean, where cruise ships were anchored, and where pine trees, cacti, and the unblocked view of the horizon were beyond awesome. It is also rich in history. Our motor coach traversed the Grand Corniche that was built by Napoleon and follows the ancient Aurelian Way. We stopped at the picturesque village of La Turbie, where we admired a sweeping panorama over the Mediterranean and the Principality of Monaco.

Grande Corniche view of the Mediterranean and Monaco

Pine trees on the homes along the narrow road of the corniche

Our group enjoyed delightful Provençal specialties of the French Riviera in the unique atmosphere of La Bergerie Restaurant in the French Alps. We proceeded down to Monaco from where we could see the top of the pine-forested Alps. This was one of the best experiences I treasure. I can't exchange the true joy I felt in my heart. ("Les Trois Corniches: 3 Roads Carved into the Mountainside," https://www.dangerousroads.org/europe/france/8810-les-trois-corniches.html).

In Florence, Italy, our walking tour took us to the Cathedral de Santa Maria del Fiore (the Duomo), Signoria Square, and Santa Croce Basilica. We enjoyed the views of Florence from Piazzale Michelangelo.

In Venice, the first thing was a scrumptious Italian dinner. Then we had romantic gondola serenade while on journey on the Grand Canal, passing by magnificent and elegant palaces. Thereafter, a canal cruise by private launch to St. Mark's Square and a visit to a glass-blowing factory. Tony and I did not go with the suggested optional tour of Murano Island. We decided to explore La Serenissima, a name for the Republic of Venice. It existed for 1,100 years, from the late seventh century until 1797, when it was conquered by Napoleon. ("Republic of Venice," *Wikipedia*, https://en.wikipedia.org/wiki/Republic_of_Venice)

Cars were strictly banned there. There are no roads, but just footpaths and canals. Crossing the Rialto Bridge (Ponte di Rialto), the oldest of four bridges spanning the Grand Canal, we went to St. Mark's Square, visited Antonio Vivaldi's Museum, and got myself a CD of his violin concerto "The Four Seasons." Finally, we ate at a Chinese restaurant after an almost exhausting walk around labyrinth footpaths with shops offering various merchandise and souvenir items. It was a satisfying lunch of Chinese food with an Italian twist. Instead of Chinese rice noodles, it was made with thin spaghetti. It still tasted like a Chinese dish anyway.

Off to Rome we went. We passed over the Apennine Mountains and through the Umbria region of rolling hills and the medieval city of Orvieto, which is situated on a volcanic rock.

Rome is truly an impressive city. We joined an optional walking tour conducted by a local tour guide, who was an expert in history. It started with an evening stroll on the Piazza Navona, notably the most beautiful and famous public square in the center of Rome. It has three fountains: Fontana di Quattro Fiumi (Fountain of the Four Rivers), Fontana del Moro (Fountain of the Moor), and Fontana del Nettuno (Fountain of Neptune). The Fountain of the Four Rivers has an Egyptian obelisk standing just over fifty-four-and-a-quarter-feet tall. It is surrounded by four statues that represent the rivers of the continents where Christianity was spread in Africa (Nile), Europe (Danube), Asia (Ganges), and the Americas (Rio de la Plata). Surrounding this baroque-style square are examples of baroque architecture in palaces, churches, shops, and pavement cafés ("Piazza Navona," *Wikipedia* https://en.wikipedia.org/wiki/Piazza_Navona).

The Piazza della Rotonda is dominated by the Pantheon. A

pantheon is a temple of all the gods. This used to be a Roman temple but is now a Catholic church called Basilica of St. Mary and the Martyrs.

Our evening tour culminated in a delicious dinner at one of Rome's finest restaurants with a concert of typical Italian songs and bel canto, consisting of arias of long, spinning vocal phrases. Good food, good music, excellent ambience, and wonderful camaraderie. The ten Australians and nine Canadians were the most fun among the group for they drank the most wine, which made them laugh the loudest.

The most awaited part of the tour followed. Included in the package tour was a visit to St. Peter's Basilica, a stop at the Forum to admire and view the Colosseum (we were not able to go inside to explore it), and to see the Circus Maximus, where the chariot race scene in the movie *Ben Hur* was filmed.

St. Peter's Basilica

As for the free time, there was an optional tour that cost $61 each to enhance the visit to the Basilica. We joined this extended tour and saw the famous Tapestry Gallery, the Gallery of Maps, and ultimately, the Sistine Chapel, where the masterpieces of Michelangelo's genius are in full glory. The Sistine Chapel has dimensions of about 134 × 44 × 68 feet. The ceiling was painted in the Renaissance style by Michelangelo, as was the giant fresco, *The Last Judgment,* behind the altar. The Sistine Chapel is in the Apostolic Palace in Vatican City, the official residence of the pope. Originally known as the Capella Magna (Great Chapel), this chapel has served as a place of both religious and functionary papal activity. Today, it is the site of papal conclave, the process by which a new pope is elected. The Catholic faith is depicted in the arts painted in the Sistine chapel. It was amazing but not easy to view because the paintings were all over every space. One would prefer to lie on the floor to appreciate better the arts on the ceiling. I found it overwhelming ("Sistine Chapel," *Wikipedia,* https://en.wikipedia. org/wiki/Sistine_Chapel).

Another optional tour for further exploration of Rome's past was a visit to one of the catacombs where early Christians gathered to escape persecution. They were constructed and used as underground cemeteries. I found it eerie and would not do it again. Who would like to walk in narrow corridors and pass alongside places and open spaces where the dead were once buried?

The final optional tour in Rome happened during a heavy downpour. With big umbrellas, we braved the rain from the motor coach to the impressive Trevi Fountain to toss coins, wishing to be back in Rome or to find love. Then a drive along the glamorous most famous Via Vettorio Veneto, colloquially called Via Veneto (famed as the setting of the Federico Fellini's award-winning 1960 film *La Dolce Vita*), and the Piazza Venezia, with all the splendor of its monuments. Piazza Venezia is the hub of several thoroughfare intersections, like Via del Fori Imperial and Via del Corso. It is the site of the Tomb of the Unknown Soldier, Trajan's Column, Palazzo Venezia, and the Monument to Vittorio Emanuele II, among other structures ("Piazza Venezia," *Wikipedia*, https://en.wikipedia.org/wiki/Piazza_Venezia).

The fifteen-day tour of five countries and ten cities was culminated by a relaxing and enjoyable typical Italian dinner with drinks and wine in Rome. Music made the parting with new friends a little more memorable as we all joined in singing some familiar Italian songs.

The cost of this package tour and the optional side trips were funded from our savings. It was our choice to fund our retirement or to live as we love to. People have different priorities. We opted to undertake what is best for our happiness and well-being, thus this fantastic tour of Western Europe.

Chapter 8

Credit Card–Facilitated Extravagance (Justified by Gained Experiences Rich in History and Culture)

While Tony progressed in his employment with the State of Maryland in Minority Business Enterprise/Department of Transportation (MBE/DOT), I was still in the state of confusion as to what direction to take. I could do marketing, engage in this or that venture, or go back to a career in insurance and financial services. Carl was attending his computer studies at the University of Maryland College Park (UMCP), while Zarah was taking her film and television studies at NYU's Tisch School of the Arts.

The use of credit cards when income was insufficient made possible the family vacations in Puerto Rico and Canada and the ocean cruise with friends to Nassau in the Caribbeans. The credit cards facilitated our travel to Manila to lay to rest my father who passed away in Silver Spring, Maryland. It was his wish to be interred in his country of birth. Two funeral services were celebrated for him. One in Silver Spring for family and friends residing in the United States and another in Manila for our large family and friends.

It also afforded us the opportunity of visiting my sister in Canberra, Australia, when she delivered her youngest child. It also made possible our several trips to Las Vegas, Nevada, for network marketing conventions held twice at the Mandalay Bay Resort Hotel, Luxor Hotel & Casino, MGM Grand Casino. Other conferences attended with the network marketing group took place in Florida, New Jersey, New York, Virginia, Washington DC, and Maryland. After attending one of the conferences in Las Vegas, I invited my sister Agnes, who was then living in Los Angeles, to come to Las Vegas. We rented a sedan with Tony as the designated driver. He wouldn't allow me to drive when we were together. Tony, Agnes, and I spent twelve days exploring the three national parks of Grand Canyon, Bryce Canyon and the Zion, after first spending time at the Hoover Dam in Nevada, as well as Phoenix and Sedona, Arizona. These places are some of the best natural landforms on earth. We watched the sunrise and the sunset at the Grand Canyon, which were both gorgeous and captivating. Went to both the south and north rims of the Grand Canyon. We drove three hours to the Paria River confluence with the Colorado River. We saw people who went whitewater rafting.

Paria and Colorado rivers

Bryce Canyon National Park in Utah is composed of natural amphitheaters of hoodoos or pinnacles. It is like thousands and thousands of very delicate spires seen in Gothic-style churches. Zion National Park is ideal for hiking. Compared with Grand

Canyon, where you are on top when you get in the park unless you go down to the Colorado River, in Zion, you are below and look up to the giant mountains of rocks and boulders. I likened it to looking up to the tall buildings while walking along Fifth Avenue in Manhattan. Hoover Dam is a marvel of human creative power. Phoenix is the capital of Arizona. Sedona is located in a desert of red soil and made more beautiful with its red-rock mountains and red-rock buttes and canyons. The scenery is lush with vegetation and forest.

We stayed overnight in a luxurious hotel for free. I accepted an offer to listen to a presentation of time-share investment on the condition that there would be no pressure selling. I was confident I would not succumb to the sales pitch because Tony and I already had one. We woke up refreshed and ready to go for more adventure. It was in this part of the United States that I first saw a perfect rainbow across the sky.

It may seem ridiculous to have indulged in those trips and extravagant hotel accommodations when there were no funds to cover them. Looking back, the experience shared with Tony and Agnes may not have happened at all if we always worried about money. The timing was ripe, too, since it was the last convention attended in Las Vegas for my networking venture.

Three years later, after the European Spotlight tour of ten cities, Tony and I joined another fifteen-day European tour dubbed the Bohemian Highlights with same travel company. I was fascinated by European history and culture and remnants of ancient civilizations. Where possible, I preferred the personal experience instead of just imagining it from books I read. This tour took us to Berlin, Nuremberg and Frankfurt in Germany; Poznan, Warsaw, Czestochowa, Auschwitz and Krakow in Poland; Budapest and Gyor in Hungary; Vienna, Austria; and Tabor, Prague and Pilsen in Czech Republic.

The fall of the Berlin Wall (German *masuerfall*) on November

9, 1989, was a pivotal event in world history, marking the fall of the Iron Curtain and the start of the fall of communism in Eastern and Central Europe. The fall of the inner German border took place shortly afterwards. An end to the cold war was declared at the Malta Summit three weeks later. German reunification took place in October of the following year. The fall occurred five days after half a million people gathered in East Berlin in a mass protest at the Berlin Wall dividing communist East Germany from West Germany ("Fall of the Berlin Wall," *Wikipedia,* https://en.wikipedia.org/wiki/Fall_of_the_Berlin_Wall).

After World War II, defeated Germany was divided up by the United States, France and the Soviet Union, which occupied the eastern part. East Germany, known as the German Democratic Republic, became the Soviet Union's foothold in Western Europe. Berlin was split four ways. British, French and American zones held the west of the city, and a Soviet zone occupied the east. West Berlin became an island surrounded by communist East Germany. In 1961, to prevent people from East Berlin from fleeing to the west, a wall was built ("The Berlin Crisis, 1958–1961," Office of the Historian, https://history.state.gov/milestones/1953-1960/berlin-crises).

We visited the famous Wall of Freedom, the only sizable part of the wall still standing, the remnant of Berlin's "Tale of Two Cities." We saw the part of the double wall where people unsuccessfully tried to escape, resulting in their deaths. There were success stories, too, like when they overcame the treacherous route of scaling the double wall and then finally crossing the canal to reach the West Berlin side and freedom. They were no longer shot at by the East German guards. But before reaching the imaginary boundary of the canal, life could still be snuffed by a guard's bullet.

We viewed spectacular landmarks on both sides of the former wall. We visited the German Parliament Building, the *Reichstag.* It has become the symbol of the reunited Berlin. The dome exemplifies ultramodern architecture. It is a very impressive structure made of glass, letting in lots of natural light. We took the elevator up to the dome and walked down the spiral staircase for a much better view and easier descent.

Another landmark we visited was Checkpoint C—more commonly called Checkpoint Charlie by the Americans. This iconic symbol of the cold war is located on the historic street of *Friedrichstrase*, in the American-occupied city center. Checkpoint C is one of several crossings in and around Berlin. The others are checkpoints Alpha and Bravo. Checkpoint Charlie is the only gateway where East Germany allowed Allied diplomats, military personnel, and foreign tourists to pass into Berlin's Soviet sector. It was the site of many incidents that could have altered history. One such incident was an infamous showdown between the United States and the USSR, triggered when a US diplomat was not allowed to enter East Berlin to attend the opera, and the continued denial of Americans' entry to East Berlin. The United States moved ten M-48 tanks into position around Checkpoint Charlie. The East German Soviet allies responded by positioning thirty-three T-55 tanks at the Brandenburg Gate. Ten of these tanks continued fifty to a hundred meters from Checkpoint Charlie on the Soviet side of the sector boundary. A potential World War III was aborted with the diplomacy between US Attorney General Robert F. Kennedy and KGB spy Georgi Bolshakov.

For twenty-nine years, Checkpoint Charlie embodied the cold war. The original guardhouse is on display at the Allied Museum in Berlin. A replica was installed as a tourist attraction.

We visited Checkpoint Charlie Museum, a private museum in Berlin. It uses photographs and related documents to tell the stories of successful escape attempts. It also presents the significant events in world history, secret agent whodunnits, tragic escapes and joyful moments. People would make any necessary sacrifices and use any means to be free. There were some success stories of flight from communist Germany, of families escaping by way of homemade hot-air balloon, jumping out of windows adjacent to the wall, using meat hooks to scale the border fences, digging tunnels and swimming across the Baltic Sea. There are even stories about being smuggled in a refrigerator truck, hiding under the carcasses of slaughtered and stuffed pigs being transported to the West. https://infogalactic.com/info/ Escape attempts and victims of the inner German border.

Aboard our luxurious motor coach, the next city visited was Warsaw, Poland's seat of government. Elected kings ruled Poland from 1573 to 1795. They elected foreign monarchs from Austria, France, Russia, Germany, Denmark and Sweden. Royal elections in Poland were the elections of individual kings, rather than dynasties. In addition to the regular sessions of the general sejm (bicameral parliament) in the era of electable kings beginning in 1573, three special types of sejms (convocation, election and coronation) have handled the process of the royal election in the interregnum period. Polish Constitution of May 3, 1791 abolished the elective monarchy and turned it into hereditary monarchy and established the Polish Commonwealth in its place. "Royal elections in Poland." https://hyperleap.com/topic/ Royal elections in Poland.

"HISTORY OF POLAND." http://www.historyworld.net/ wrldhis/PlainTextHistories.asp?ParagraphID=iqq.

Currently, it is a democratic government with a president as head of state and a prime minister appointed by the president as the head of government. "What Type Of Government Does Poland Have? - WorldAtlas." 25 Apr. 2017, https://www.worldatlas.com/articles/what-type-of-government-does-poland-have.html.

The most poignant places we visited in Poland were the concentration camps Auschwitz I and Birkenau, also called

Auschwitz II. We toured several buildings where the Nazis exterminated the Jews and Poles. We saw the gas chambers that looked like showers, but instead of water, what came out of them was lethal gas. There were rooms with glass cases exhibiting hair and shoes of adults and children who were victims of the Holocaust. These concentration camps were used as the killing centers by the Nazis during World War II. Nothing much is left in Birkenau, which was the larger camp of the two, as the Nazis destroyed the buildings to hide their crimes and atrocities. It is a large ground with a fence close to where our motor coach was parked. This camp had been featured in some movies. Many people were brought to tears by what they saw. ("Auschwitz: Concentration Camp, Facts, Location—History," https://www. history.com/topics/world-war-ii/auschwitz).

I carve away at the mention of Warsaw, bearing Frederic Chopin in my mind. To me, Frederic Chopin was one of the world's top-ten composers. We were treated to an exclusive recital of Chopin's music by the celebrated Polish pianist Jwona Klimaszewska in one of Warsaw's lovely, old, summer palaces. It was raining when we visited the large bronze statue of Frederic Chopin in Lazienski Park.

Poland is also famous for the Wieliczka salt mines near the city of Krakow. We took a lift to about 1,073 feet below the ground; the length of the tunnel is 186 miles. The salt mine is over seven hundred years old. The chambers are filled with unique salt sculptures, like the glittering chandeliers made of pure salt crystals, not crystals from Murano nor the Venetian crystals. The floors, walls, and ceilings are made of salt, as are religious sculptures and reliefs and famous fairy-tale characters. It is a huge underground world that we barely scratched the surface of during our visit. "Wieliczka Salt Mines: All You Need to Know (2022)." https://krakowmonamour.com/ wieliczka-salt-mines/.

Wieliczka salt mines

As relayed by our local tour guide, and what I found amazing, was that the rock salt deposits in Wieliczka had been mined for table salt beginning in the thirteenth century. It continued to be mined until 2007, when it was fully dedicated to tourism. The sale of salt provided 30 percent of the entire kingdom's income in the times of Casimir III the Great, one of the most glorified and accomplished Polish kings.

Then it was on to Hungary. Our local tour guide was a daughter of a military man, very well-informed, and educated in the United States. Budapest, its capital, is considered by many one of the most beautiful cities.

Hungary also established a parliamentary representative democratic republic form of government. The country came under German occupation during World War II, which was followed by Soviet occupation. It was a socialist people's republic from 1949 until the fall of the Berlin Wall in 1989. Their government ran under an amended version of their 1949 constitution beginning in October 1989. They adopted a new constitution in 2011. They joined the European Union in 2004.

This was my second visit to Vienna, Austria. I was no longer enthusiastic to visit the usual tourist attractions. At St. Stephen's Cathedral, by chance, we met a Filipina, who works as a nurse in Vienna. She was excited to take us to a Filipino restaurant. We took the Vienna U-Bahn and took a short walk to the Philippine Embassy. There was a small café where we had a good fill of Philippine foods, like siopao (a bun filled with pork and carrots and peas), arroz caldo (rice chicken soup), and pansit.

Prague, Czech Republic, is another very impressive city. Czech Republic was under communist rule from 1948 until the fall of communism in 1989. They were able to establish a democratic government soon thereafter. It became a member of the European Union in 2004. We visited the usual tourist attractions like castles, cathedrals, and squares.

Tony and I lived our lives to the fullest even before retirement. We could not take the chance to wait until we had all the money anticipated we would need for retirement. After all, there was no assurance that we would be able to enjoy our youth, good health, and energy even when the coffers were full. All these opportunities were made possible by readily available financial resources supplied by credit cards. These debts could be repaid, but time and opportunity might not be there when we were ready to undertake trips.

The conventions we attended were part of our network financial service business, and we considered education a must investment for our children. Travels, trips, and adventures lift and buoy our spirits and lives. These were the forces driving me to dream further for a better life. The formula for success is not very far behind. A good balance in both our careers, family life, relationships, dreams, and the future is in order. Retirement planning is currently at hand, but we are taking a more pragmatic approach to make it totally work for us. That is the key to achieving success.

Chapter 9
Reawakening and Shaking Things Up

My former employer, Abdi Parvizian, called me up one day and asked if I could come and help him with the going out of business sale of his furniture and rug business.

Author with her husband Tony Cabanas and Abdi Parvizian

Of course, it was an opportunity to return to a regular schedule of work and income. I have learned that it was better to have W-2s, being paid a salary, and having taxes withheld rather than having to file Form 1099 as an independent contractor, thereby making employment taxes your total responsibility. Qualifying for or refinancing an existing mortgage, obtaining an auto loan, qualifying for credit cards with lower interest rates, a higher credit line and longer billing periods are often easier for employees than for independent contractors.

In agreeing to work for Abdi, I would be giving back for the many favors he did for me and my family. Abdi was mainly responsible for my immigration to the United States and for my family. Abdi's brothers Manoucher and Gus also provided assistance by allowing me to work in their businesses in Fairfax, Virginia and Houston, Texas. I must acknowledge the brilliant advice of Massud, the brother who runs the business in Dallas, Texas. He pointed out the options before me, such as where to settle with my family. He made sure that I stayed in metro Washington DC area for my children's education and its living conditions. I can't thank him enough for sharing his acumen.

Being a seasoned businessman, Abdi partnered with a nationally recognized liquidator. The operation was huge, and a lot of people were involved in the process. I was tasked to monitoring the inventory and review the weekly financial reports from the liquidators. I began by hiring my friend's two sons and the son of another friend to work as data entry staff for inventory control. These kids were computer savvy, fast and hardworking. It was summer and a timely arrangement for everyone.

I learned it was not only existing inventory that was liquidated but new inventory as well. I was energized and did a good job supervising the staff doing the inventory control. I was paid well, and on top of that, Abdi was generous with regular bonuses. The liquidators were aware of my role and presented me with well-prepared financial reports. On several occasions, while reviewing and analyzing these reports, I found irregularities where profits were hidden. I reported them to Abdi, and corrections were made. I thought that was more than enough to have earned my pay.

It was then that I heard my wake-up call and was called to face the mirror. I began assessing the pros and cons of my career. I put to use my many years of work experience in accounting and positions I held in various levels of corporate organizations and industries. In addition, my degree in law and admission to the Philippine bar boosted my professional insights. I practiced corporate law, consultancy in labor, employment placement, and agency relations. Because of various employment possibilities, I was distracted from what I could do best and failed to realize my best potential. I had delved into marketing most types of insurance and worked in mutual funds, variable insurance and annuities. I had also obtained a license as a financial adviser. I attended seminars in flipping real estate, invested in materials for grants from federal government, options trading and cost reduction service business. I did not pursue the practice of law in the United States as it would require an enormous investment of time and money. I turned away from this course of action as it would be funded again by loans and credit cards. Until I confronted this crossroad, once more facilitated by Abdi, I made a decision on what career I would place my focus.

The sale was completed successfully. And thanks to Abdi, another window of opportunity opened. Abdi told me that another company needed my services. For the next thirteen years, until my retirement, I worked there.

Chapter 10
Sophisticated Auction Industry

The sophisticated auction industry was totally different from all the experiences I had in over five decades of working. It has its own culture and language. It dealt in fine arts, which included paintings, sculptures, prints, antique furniture and fixtures, jewelry, Asian and Oriental arts, manuscripts, other antiquities and collectibles, and real estate. I did not have the exposure in handling or getting to know the lots, items, or merchandise that the company dealt with. That field belongs to those in the operations department, like the specialists and appraisers. I don't know the mechanics of valuing art objects, paintings, or antiquities.

I was the chief financial officer (CFO) of Sloans & Kenyon Auctioneers and Appraisers, a premier auction house in the Washington DC area. On consolidating her ownership of the company, the president, Stephanie A. Kenyon, reorganized the corporation. She terminated some employees, and I assisted her in filling those positions. I brought in someone I previously helped transition from a position to one related to the degree she earned in college. She now had years of good experience, so I invited her. Mildred Abana joined me in this new company on a part-time basis. She turned out to be well suited for the business office. She had excellent customer-relations skills. I hired a friend of Mildred's, who was a full-time mother and wife. She had a degree in business management and excellent skills in handling difficult clients. Evangeline Ricamata could turn in arrogant and ill-mannered consignors to pleasant and considerate clients. She worked full time and was available to work during auctions held on Saturdays and Sundays or holidays. To take charge of the Consignment Boutique and Gallery, the retail section of the business, Remy Aquino was the perfect choice. In due time, she was ready to take up the cudgels as its manager. Her customer relations and selling skills were excellent. Even now, whenever I go to the Consignment Boutique and Gallery, I always leave happy with purchases of some trinkets and fancy articles as good finds.

While at this company, I let go of the bookkeeper from an employment agency. I hired another who was recommended to me and seemed to be qualified. After less than a year, I fired her for reasons of trust and bad attitude. I needed a good accountant-bookkeeper and hired Johan Gunawan. I had known him for over fifteen years; he was then my assistant in another company. I was just not sure if he would accept the position since he was a successful realtor at this time. A part-time work arrangement was agreed upon. Johan worked in the office three days a week and three or four days for his real estate business. This arrangement was mutually beneficial. He was a typical accountant, very detailed and always completed on schedule. He came on time and dressed sharply and cleanly. His manners were pleasant, and he got along well with the other staff members and employees. Johan took over as the company's CFO when I retired. To this day, the team I assembled for the auction company is still together. However, it's worth to mention that the person one can consult on about anything other than accounting is Ellen Garrity. She's the go-to person at Sloans.

Sloans & Kenyon Auction Company

Most people are intimidated of buying and selling at auctions. The industry is different, and it is not common to find auction companies around the corner like retail stores. Here are some salient points I learned during my thirteen years in the industry.

What you should know and do before putting an item in an auction:

- A dealer or collector should make sure it is appraised by a professional. On a free appraisal day, specialists can do a verbal appraisal. For written appraisal, there is a fee.
- Contact a specialist of your particular item. If the item is large or heavy, send a picture and description. Based on the specialist's expertise and research, the specialist can make an appraisal or may come to take a look at your item and then provide an appraisal.
- If the item is worth auctioning, you may consign it to the auction company subject to its rules and conditions. It will be scheduled for auction.

- All items or lots are exhibited for a week. Interested buyers can leave their bids on any lot or lots of their choice before the auction.
- Items for auction are listed on the company website and auction site of a contracted online marketplace.

To take part in an auction:

- Register and get a bid card with a number. It is like an ID card. There is no cost for it.
- To bid on a lot, raise the card to show to the auctioneer, who then acknowledges your bid.
- The auctioneer will increase the bidding price in regular increments as long as there are bidders.
- The auctioneer will warn if there are any more bids.
- If no other bid is placed, the auctioneer bangs the gavel. Yours is the winning bid if it is the last bid.

What a bidder pays for the purchase:

- The winning bid.
- The auction company's premium of 10 percent (more or less, depending on the object's value).
- Sales tax
- Shipping and handling fees, if applicable.

The consignor is paid the winning bid for his sold lot minus:

- The auction company's sales commission, ranging from 20 percent to 50 percent on average. This is subject to negotiation depending on the appraised value of the lot.
- Any cost of agreed repair or retouch.
- Any shared or exclusive advertising or promotional costs.

There are several ways to bid, even if they are not in attendance; this includes in another country. Among them are:

- Directly from the gallery.
- Absentee bidding by leaving bids on any lots during the exhibitions prior to the auction in person.
- Sending an absentee bid form by fax, stating the lot or lots and amount of bid.
- Sending an intent to bid form by phone. Phone bidding assistants will call when the items are ready for bidding.
- Online through the company's website.
- An online auction site or marketplace as contracted by the auction company.

There were times when the bidding was so intense. It occurs when a lot is offered at an attractive value, an artwork by a famous artist, or when it has a provenance. Bidders compete ferociously, and bids often go beyond expectations. It is such an exciting scene. I enjoyed being on the phone to help bidders.

On the one hand, some collectors think what they have is a treasure trove and put an unreasonable value of expectation on the items that no one would bid at the auction. It is part of human nature to think that your collection is truly valuable and special. In reality, they may not be unless you have a good training in appraisal yourself or have them appraised by a professional. On the other hand, there are lots that are nominally valued, but many dealers or collectors would compete on them, raising bids to an astonishing price. There is a total opposite expectation in an auction. The consignor of an item expects to have many bidders to compete on an item, while on the other hand, the collector or dealer would bid in the hope of getting something at a bargain price. What you get for an item sold at an auction is usually about a third of the retail price. It's still a good deal.

Some items from estates to be auctioned off are amazing in the sense that they are very personal to the owners. Sometimes you find awards of distinction from international and famous organizations, photographs of distinguished people and celebrities, and family and personal collectibles. I wonder why the heirs did not bother to keep them. I have a friend who collected a sizable number of Asian jars, vases, and ornaments and told her daughter she could have them. The daughter replied, "Mom, give them to my brother."

Some of these unsold items and those not taken back by their consignors were trashed or donated to charity after a certain period. I did not become a collector of things but rather a collector of memories through travel. I did not wish to spend my money in these goods, except for jewelry. They are investments, especially the ones with history, are original pieces of art, and come from interesting or important places of origin. Jewelry appealed to me for the simple reason that you can enjoy it right away. They are easy to handle, not bulky, and children can keep them. These are simply personal choices and preferences. Jewelry can be redesigned or recut to make it fit to your liking. One time I opted to buy from the auction some jewelry worth the equivalent of my IRA contribution for that year. I did not regret it.

What I learned from this experience was that one man's trash is another man's treasure. As a kid, I was never a collector except for some stamps and coins. I found out that a great number of people would consign for auction multifarious objects that you might consider useless or valueless. Old and used rugs and furniture and paintings I considered ugly to my untrained eye would sometimes surprisingly sell for incredulous sums of money.

Collecting art is an investment, a hobby, or a passion. Whatever your motivation, it can be worth your while.

Chapter 11
Project Tax Break: Second Purchase

I had yet to know Johan Gunawan's caliber as a real estate agent. He owned several rental properties. He would tell me of properties available in my neighborhood and in the vicinity that I might be interested in. I became curious, and one Saturday, we went to see some of the properties. Most of them he showed me were listings of other real estate agents. In short, he was more of a buyer's agent, not the seller's agent. He worked hard to find properties on the market and offered them to his contacts. He also had listings of his own. He had made several closings, so he was a relatively successful agent. His approach was soft and gentle, always with a ready smile or a light laugh.

In my association with Johan, I had started to get interested in the real estate market. One interesting thing I learned was that real estate had long been a path to wealth. I read about lives of people who had successful careers and made money in real estate. They started small in real estate, and then diversified their investments in riskier ventures that required more capital, like franchising, commercial real estate, and multiunit buildings. The real estate business does not require a lot of initial investment. To qualify to buy a home, you must be currently employed, have a good income as shown on your W-2, income tax returns, a good credit score, and a relatively nominal down payment.

I also became aware of the neighborhoods and how property values were affected by factors that I never thought would matter at all. Johan always had information on real estate available in the area. He went to open houses and checked out and compared values. He relayed to me which ones were good buys and those that were not and why.

My mind started to wander, and I not only dreamed at night but also during the day, envisioning the way out of our debts and to a bright tomorrow. What motivated me to address this debt crisis? There were many reasons. First was to live debt-free so we could breathe fully and be truly happy. Would it not be fun to have peace of mind and not to worry about debts piling up because of continued borrowing and accumulating more debt because of high interest rates on unpaid balances? Second, we could have the retirement program we wanted for ourselves but had put off for immediate desires. I imagined myself and Tony having a retirement income that could sustain us during our golden years. Third and many more, to fund our children's weddings, celebrations with families, reunions, travels, charities, legacies, and savings that would boost our self-confidence and self-respect.

Tony and I were motivated to provide for our needs and wants. Our children had graduated and were gainfully employed. Both of us still had full-time employment and had learned to understand the burden of paying more taxes than we used to. Tony would put more into his 401(k) and 401(a) accounts necessary to be matched by the state of Maryland. In addition, we needed to do some planning to save on payment of taxes. We only put money into the IRA or 401(k) when it was necessary to minimize payment of taxes. We did not have investments in the stock market, CDs, or mutual funds. We both had variable universal life policies. There is a cash value, but it is not at a fixed rate. Rather, it is invested in underlying subaccounts in the stock market. We took out the same for our children.

I talked to Johan about the tax issue. One weekend he told me he had a property I should see. He took me to a subdivision less than a mile from my house. What impressed me was its size. It was a corner lot located in a very good school district, a few steps from the bus stop, within walking distance to a metro station, and located between two town centers. How about the selling price? On December 30, 2008, the Case-Shiller Home-Price index reported its largest price drop in its history. The credit crisis resulting from the bursting of the housing bubble was an important cause of the great recession in the United States; this real estate bubble affected over half of the States. In late January 2007, the average thirty-year fixed rate was 6.25 percent. In 2009, it decreased by 1.5 percent, to 5.10 percent, resulting in a free fall in home prices. By September 29, 2008, the stock market crashed. The Dow Jones Industrial Average fell 777.68 points ("2,997 pts. drop in March 16, 2020," *Statista Research Dept.*). Economic recessions typically bring low interest rates and create a buyers' market for single-family homes. A downturn can be an opportune time to buy a home. When the Federal Reserve raised the federal funds rate, it sent adjustable mortgage interest rates skyrocketing. As a result, home values plummeted, and borrowers defaulted.

The main culprit of this crisis was deregulation in the financial industry and supervision. It permitted banks to engage in hedge-fund trading using derivatives. When the values of the derivatives crumbled, banks stopped lending to each other. The benefit to recession is inflation rates tend to fall, which can benefit those on fixed incomes or reliant on cash savings. It also tackles long-term inflationary pressures. For example, in 1980–1981, recession helped reduce the high inflation rates of the 1970s ("Financial Crisis of 2007–2008," *Wikipedia*, https://en.wikipedia.org/wiki/ Financial_crisis_of_2007%E2%80%932008).

Johan told me that the seller's brokers were accepting bids that would be closed in two days. I could not believe he would put me in this rush. He had told several people in the office, but no one paid attention to it or showed any interest in it. *Can I afford it?* I wondered. First of all, during the recession, the prices of single-family homes were down and interest rates were low. Homeowners defaulted on their mortgages, which created a buyer's market. I had good credit and a decent income. Johan checked to see if I qualified. He suggested that I join my sister Agnes as a co-buyer, and we submitted a bid. After a week, Johan told me we won by a slim margin.

In the course of time, the previously gloomy old house had new doors, a new air conditioner and heater, new flooring, fresh paint, a new roof, a new washer and dryer, and a new kitchen and appliances. The lower level had more windows and renovated living space. As co-owners, I claim the tax deductions, and my sister has lived in the house ever since. That was about twelve years ago.

Having addressed a problem and expecting to have a good tax refund, we anticipated funds for the grand reunion that was in the planning stage for a year. We had to go through this huge undertaking. How about my retirement fund? It can wait, can't it? Maybe.

Chapter 12
Strategy: Stay Clear from Debts

The time came when having excessive debts caused a serious concern with Tony and me. We started to face the realities of our lives. We had some good income, but most of it went to financing our accumulated debts. What about if we didn't have debts? We could start to accumulate wealth and have funds for our retirement. Tony and I decided to get out of debt. How we went about it required a lot of serious self-discipline and a paradigm shift. To build wealth, we had to do the following:

1. Earn good income, maintain it, and possibly increase it.
2. Pay off debts.
3. Have passive income, like rentals, residual commissions, or interest from investments.
4. Be smart spenders.
5. Be an economic, not a wasteful consumer.
6. Be mindful of our cashflow in and cashflow out.

First, we took inventory of our assets and our debts to determine our net worth. At the time, it was totally a negative balance. However, we had our one and only asset that could be the succor of our agony. Homeownership has far greater financial benefits than the initial challenges and headaches of finding the right home to fit one's requirements, the qualifying process, and money for the down payment and closing costs. Laura Mueller, from *moving.com*, shares five benefits of homeownership with which I agree.

1. Build up a stronger financial future—Owning a home is one of the fundamental means of accumulating wealth as we age. Asset-wealth is a much more secure predictor of future financial stability than income, which can—and often does, in today's evolving economy, home values generally increase by 3% to 4% every year, thanks to inflation and natural population growth. I strongly agree and did this strategy in the accumulation of wealth.

2. Home ownership tax deductions—The interest and property tax of mortgaged properties are deductible for income tax purposes. The mortgage points on the loan can be written off from income taxation. These deductions we need more than ever as our fixed income from salaries are growing. But compare that with its purchasing power. You will note that due to inflation a $100 a year ago will no longer allow you to buy the same.

3. Amass equity—Equity in your home builds as the value of your home increases, and equity builds as you pay more of your loan. Fortunately, in just 5 years the appraised value of our first home had increased by 63%. Every time we pay our mortgage, the expense portion is only the interest and the property tax. The payment on the principal is a saving kept in the equity. Compare that with rent of an apartment. All the rent is expense. We were apartment renters for 9 long years.

4. More control over day-to-day housing related costs—Unless you change the terms of your mortgage, you know the base cost that you're going to be spending to live in your home every month, both now and in the future. This affords more stability than rent, which is variable and can (and often does) change over time. As a homeowner, you can make better short- or long-term financial decisions that are geared specifically toward your own financial goals.

5. Positive perks—A mortgage is considered "good debt" and as such, it is likely to increase your credit score, provided you always make your payment on time. It also improves your credit-worthiness for other things you may want to consider, like a business loan or new line of credit ("5 Big Financial Benefits of Home Ownership," *Moving.com,* August 22, 2018, https://www.moving.com/tips/5-big-financial-benefits-of-home-ownership/).

The aspiration to be debt-free was encouraged by the accumulation of equity in our humble single-family home. Within just two years from date of purchase, the value of the property increased by 19 percent. With the knowledge of the impact of compounding interest on debts, we deemed it appropriate to refinance our mortgage from the original 8.5 percent to 7.25 percent, a savings of 1.25 percent. This strategy lowered the monthly cash outflow on our monthly amortization.

To further improve our debt management, we consolidated our credit card debt, which carried a much higher interest, averaging 15.70 percent, by a second mortgage at the rate of 11.99 percent. We paid a total of $46,050 to Chase, Advanta, a second Chase card, First USA, Citibank, American Express, and Visa. Consolidating high-interest credit card debts to one fixed monthly payment improved further our cash flow. As a result, we had zero liabilities to credit card companies. And moreover, we had a favorable debt-to-income ratio.

Based on this cleaning up of our debts, do you think we learned our lessons fast? Not quite.

One could expect that after paying these debts, we could live debt-free. But it was quite the contrary. Our debts ballooned from zero to six figures within five years. Our incomes had increased, but our debts had accumulated from various missteps, bad financial habits, wrong decisions, and the travel itch. Our priorities were misplaced too. For these reasons, we were totally in a financial mess again.

Luckily, three years after the last refinance, the appraised value of our home had increased by 63 percent. We took advantage of a low mortgage rate and refinanced from 7.25 percent to 6.75 percent. It was amazing that this property was now appraised at more than double the original purchase price. We decided to refinance again, this time at 6.125 percent to pay off the various credit card debts as follows:

Credit Card Company	Amount Paid
Citi	$18,323
Amex	$14,247
Chase Manhattan	$13,656
Fleet	$12,958
First USA	$12,490
Discover	$6,645
MBNA America	$5,853
Wells Fargo	$5,527
Community	$5,247
Fair Finance	$3,002
Riggs National	$2,258
Amex	$2,111
Total	$102,317

Becoming aware of where we were heading, we took notice and researched the good habits of self-made millionaires. I read Thomas J. Stanley's, *The Millionaire Mind* and *The Millionaire Next Door*. We tried to emulate the habits and conduct of the rich, hoping that someday, with some good luck—like winning the lottery big time— we could experience a reversal of fortune.

Chapter 13

A Grand Family Reunion in the Philippines

Holding a family reunion in 2010 was precipitated by my idea to hold a celebration for my sixtieth birthday and our thirty-third wedding anniversary, which both fall in January. I planned to invite close friends and hold a party in one of the hotels in Washington DC. Why would I do that? To celebrate me and us? I am not into holding parties in my honor or on my behalf. So why then? Why not host a party for our families and relatives in the Philippines instead. Why not use the cost of the Washington DC event for a grand family reunion in the Philippines? Should the venue be in a Philippine hotel?

Some of the relatives in the Philippines might not come because they would have to spend for the required attire, which would be semiformal, and for hotel accommodations. Some might not even have enough for transportation costs. Tony went online and checked out possible reunion venues. He found out that a friend held their reunion in a resort near metro Manila. We liked two venues, and we asked my brother to bring his family to check out the resorts. It was a treat from us. One of the resorts was highly recommended, and we decided to concentrate on that plan. We had a year to plan for this big event.

My brother fortunately or unfortunately accepted an overseas job. When planning a family event, family members suggested different ideas as to dates, venues, foods, and every other detail, which were all conflicting. You can't move on without stress and distractions.

Since Tony and I were footing the bills, we could call the shots and need not consult any of our relatives. During this time, our incomes were stabilized, particularly mine since I took a full-time position in 2005. But how would we make preparations for an event when we are 8,571 miles from Manila?

We contracted an event planner, Irene, to arrange for a successful grand family reunion. We directed and consulted with her, who was very knowledgeable and competent. She made us a good budget and a good estimate of the costs of venue, food, overnight accommodations, and breakfasts at the Hot Springs Resort in Pansol, Calamba, Laguna. It is fewer than 50 miles from Manila. Based on the budget, we could provide transportation for relatives from Camarines Sur in the Bicol region.

The Philippines is divided into seventeen regions. There are 7,641 islands in the Philippines, of which around 2,000 islands are inhabited. One of the eight most beautiful regions is the Southern Luzon area. It is comprised of two regions: (1) Calabarzon, bordering metro Manila to the north and east. The reunion venue is in this region, and (2) the Bicol region, comprised of offshore islands ("Philippines," *Simple English Wikipedia: The Free Encyclopedia,* https://simple.wikipedia.org/wiki/Philippines). "Regions of the Philippines – PhilAtlas." https://www.philatlas.com/regions.html. This is where you can find Mayon Volcano, the symmetrical, almost perfectly conical active volcano.

Mayon Volcano in Bicol Philippines

The Hot Springs Resort is located at the foot of Mount Makiling in Laguna. The resort is also a conference venue. It has large halls that could accommodate two hundred to three hundred people, and a good number of hotel rooms and cottages to provide lodging. It can provide food and drinks, and there is a twenty-four-hour restaurant within the facility. There are large free-flowing hot springs swimming pools. In addition, around the hotel buildings and cottages located in the large vicinity of the facility, are smaller hot spring pools. Some hotel rooms have an indoor swimming pool that can be turned on when requested. There are game rooms that guests can enjoy Ping-Pong, billiards, and other games. There are obstacle courses and group game areas.

We mobilized the relatives in our hometown of Sipocot, in Naga City, and other barrios in Camarines Sur. They were tasked to register relatives who planned to attend. In order to make everyone feel a sense of belonging, we provided T-shirts to those who registered. A brother and another relative were assigned to

arrange for the transportation and ordering and printing of the
reunion T-shirts. This was the first grand reunion of the clan. No
guests, government officials, or prominent persons of the area were
invited. The reunion was strictly limited to immediate Baldoza and
Buenaobra families only.

However, the Perciano and Cabanas families were informed
through Tony's mother and sister. Their list was probably a quarter
of the total attendees. Nothing much to be worried or concerned
about this group. We just had to reimburse their fares instead of
arranging for their transportation. The Percianos were from the
Cagayan region and Cabanases were originally from Batanes Islands
in Northern Luzon. Northern Luzon is also considered one the most
beautiful regions in the Philippines.

Meanwhile, the planner regularly communicated with me by
email and cell phone calls. "Since the grand reunion is on New
Year's Eve, why not have fireworks?" Irene asked. Sure, why not. She
sent by internet the different firework designs, how many minutes
each lasted, and the costs associated with each choice. That was
cool and exciting. Since it was still Christmastime, how about
presents and a program? How about lunch and snacks on arrival
of the guests. Party was scheduled for 6:00 p.m. Dinner would be
provided and breakfast too on New Year's Day—all as part of the
package. Irene asked, "Do you require a priest to officiate a mass
before the party? How about party decorations, table settings, etc.?"
Irene was on top of everything, covering it all. She was a great
reliever of stress.

Zarah and her friend left New York for the Philippines three days
ahead of us. Carl and his fiancée left from Washington DC a day
later, and Tony and I left from Baltimore Washington International
Airport on the same day. We all stayed in the same condominium
hotel in Makati City, a part of the metro Manila area, the financial
capital of the Philippines. Morgan Baldoza Thomas, my niece,

also came from London, England, with her friend. They came a week early and were already enjoying El Nido, a resort town in the province of Palawan, famous for its white beaches, coral reefs, and as the gateway to a group of islands with cliffs and fish-filled waters, dive sites, and a long tunnel leading to an underwater cavern.

Early on December 31, our families started arriving at the venue. How excited they were to see families and relatives they hadn't seen for ages. Relatives from the Bicol region came on two big tourist buses. They started early, so they had time to spend a few hours on one of the beaches along Asian Highway 26, also known as Pan Philippine Highway.

Registration and assignment of hotel rooms went smoothly. Relatives also brought food for sharing during lunch. We had a kitchen in which some relatives prepared food such as grilled fish and vegetables. My sister Eden had a whole lechon (roasted pig) delivered. It was a feast before the party. Others opted to test the hot springs' free-flowing pool, and some just started having a party right away.

At 4:30 p.m., we distributed the T-shirts to those who registered. Those who just joined were still welcomed. The priest said the mass in anticipation for the new year. We had recognized the relatives, and that our children, Carl and Zarah, were related to all those present from my side of the family, Buenaobra and Baldoza, and from their daddy's side, the Percianos and Cabanases.

At 5:30, everyone was ushered to the huge party room for a sit-down dinner. It was decorated in festive Christmas décor. There was a podium and audio and music equipment. There were singing and dancing and a short program that included the recognition of the three grandmothers who were present. Coming from California were my eighty-five-year-old mother, Juliana Buenaobra Baldoza, and her sister, Naty Buenaobra Montemayor, who was seventy-nine years old. She is my dear aunt, who took care of me when I was a baby. And she still cares for me. My mother in-law, Lourdes Perciano Cabanas, lived in Manila, and she was eighty-eight years old. They were the survivors of their generation.

Grand Family Reunion venue

My brother Victor, who had worked in Hong Kong for thirteen years, came with some giveaway tech products for a raffle. He hadn't expected that this event would come to fruition. Out of nine living siblings in my family, six were present. Tony's only living sibling, Luz Cabanas Ramos, and her children and grandchildren were also there. Some relatives we had not seen for over four decades were there, and the reunion was more of a happy getting-to-know-you event. A cousin told me it was the only event where she was able to see all her children in one place.

Cousins from metro Manila showed apparently more progressive lives than some of those from the other regions. Some of them were driving expensive cars and SUVs.

My sisters—Eve Baldoza-Thomas from Bryce Resort, Basye, Virginia and Agnes from Silver Spring, Maryland—brought gift packages of chocolates and goodies from the duty-free shops and distributed them in addition to the shirts, pants, accessories, cosmetics, perfumed lotions, and toys brought over from the United States. We also handed out cash prizes for the singing and dance contests.

Right after the party and the distribution of gifts, we went out to watch the fireworks display. These fireworks were of colorful designs, like fountains, roman candles, Catherine wheels, and mines. It lasted for twenty-five minutes. Some cousins brought some firecrackers and sparklers that added to a more exciting evening. It was amazing, and everyone enjoyed the evening. Tony and I looked at each other and understood that this was a great idea and a fantastic decision.

The party at the pavilion ended, but the party was not over. They went swimming, playing and talking; the camaraderie continued. At our own hotel area, we invited our brothers and sisters to come and join us for a night cap. We introduced Laurence, Carl's fiancée, to our immediate family members. We had many stories about the family to share for there are ten Baldoza siblings from one set of parents. We had a fun time sampling balut. It is a delicacy and a specialty. It's a duck's egg with day-old embryo. It is boiled and eaten with a little bit of fine salt while it's hot. It is tasty and delicious. Beer is the best pairing for it.

In the early morning, the Bicol group was ready to leave after breakfast. The two tourist buses still had the banner on its side and back that said, "Buenaobra Baldoza Perciano Cabanas Grand Reunion, December 31, 2009, and January 1, 2010."

Reunion tour buses from Bicol

Everyone bade goodbyes and exchanged email addresses, phone numbers and mail addresses. They again did a side trip, this time to Manila, where they toured the Rizal Park and the Manila Bay area. To some of them, it was their first visit to the capital city.

We ate our pre-reunion meals and New Year's Day lunch at the resort's twenty-four-hour restaurant. It is famous for its fried chicken and Philippine dishes.

Then we all went to our condo-hotel in Makati City, where we checked out and went on our ways. Carl, Laurence, Zarah, and her friend left for Coron Island in the province of Palawan. It offers limestone karst landscapes, pristine beaches, crystal-clear freshwater lakes, and shallow-water coral reefs. Morgan and company left for home to London. The rest of the family stayed and continued their visit around the Manila area.

My sisters, Eve and Agnes, and my aunt Naty voluntarily and generously contributed to the cost of this first and only grand reunion. It felt good that I got that bonus from them. In addition to the cost of the grand reunion party, the guest hotel accommodations, the cost of T-shirts, the cost of two tourist buses, the bus fare reimbursements, the fireworks, the prizes, and the presents, and incorporating our airfare costs, hotel bookings, transportation costs in Manila, and our meals and expenses for the event, the total could be dumbfounding. To some people, it would be foolish to spend that money to hold the grand reunion. But for Tony and me, it was the greatest feeling of happiness to gather everyone in our families at one place at one moment of time. When will this ever happen again?

There you are, our retirement funding. We're facing the fact we need money for retirement. But it's just not the time yet. As Tony always says, "There is time for everything."

Tony and I continued our visit in the Philippines to celebrate in private my birthday and our wedding anniversary. We went to the island of Bohol, in the Central Visayas region. It is known for coral reefs and unusual geological formations. We stayed in Bohol Beach Club, which is located on Panglao Island. It is an impressive world-class resort offering guests topnotch service and facilities, along with privacy and space. It has a private, powdery-white sand beach with pristine blue waters and an unobstructed view of the sunrise. The resort provides guests with a variety of traditional Filipino foods and international cuisines. There are two large pools, one located where you can see the blue waters of Bohol Sea and the glimmering white sand beach. The other is in an area surrounded by tropical trees, flowering plants, and colorful shrubs and bushes. Nearby are guest cottages, a small restaurant, and a boutique shop.

We joined a local tour and went to the Philippine Tarsier and Wildlife Sanctuary, where we saw the world's smallest primates, the tarsiers. They have big, round eyes. They are nocturnal and feed primarily on insects. The tour included a visit to the Chocolate

Hills, as many as 1,776 hills spread over an area of around 50 square kilometers, or 12,355 acres. There are about 1,200 of these symmetrical mounds that turned cocoa-brown in the dry season, contrasting them with the surrounding greenery and verdant woods. What beautiful scenery it created ("Chocolate Hills," *Wikipedia*, https://en.wikipedia.org/wiki/Chocolate_Hills).

A memorable experience was the Loboc River Buffet Cruise. Aboard this floating restaurant, we feasted on a scrumptious buffet of local dishes while passing along the jade-green Loboc River, which is one of the cleanest rivers in the country. The floating restaurant stops on the pier by the riverside for guests to watch and/or participate in a short cultural show of dance and music. I participated in a short dance of tinikling. It is dancing in between two bamboo poles by hopping and not getting caught between the poles. The dancer looks like he or she is imitating a bird called a tikling by hopping in and out of the two poles, while two people are beating, tapping, and sliding the poles together. It surprised me to have retained my skill even after several decades. I survived without my foot being caught between the bamboo poles.

There were other points of interest that we passed, like the human-made Forest of Bilar and Loboc.

It is a 1.24 miles (or 2 kilometers) road in the Bohol Forest that is planted with mahogany trees. The road is canopied by these magnificent trees that are large, semi-evergreen, and almost all the same height. It was planted about fifty years ago as part of a reforestation project. It is a beautiful place to relax and reconnect with nature ("Bohol Man-Made Forest—a UNIQUE ..." *Daily Travel Pill*, October 6, 2020, https://dailytravelpill.com/bilar-lobo c-man-made-mahogany-forest-bohol/).

Another interesting visit was to the historical Blood Compact Shrine, or Sandugo (Visayan word meaning "one blood'). The Sandugo was a blood compact made on the island of Bohol between the Spanish explorer Miguel López de Legazpi and Datu

Sikatuna, the chieftain of Bohol on March 16, 1565. The pact was to seal their friendship and was part of the tribal tradition. This is considered the first treaty of friendship between the Spaniards and Filipinos ("," *Wikipedia*, https://en.wikipedia.org/wiki/Sandugo). "SANDUGO... Kahulugan - TAGALOG LANG." 16 Nov. 2021, https://www.tagaloglang.com/sandugo/.

It must be noted that Spanish explorers led by Ferdinand Magellan landed on the island of Homonhon on March 17, 1521, and claimed the Philippine archipelago in the name of Philip II of Spain, hence the root name of the country. The Philippines was explored and colonized forty-four years later. Spanish colonization and rule started in 1565 by Miguel López de Legazpi and ended in 1898, during the Philippine revolution and the Spanish–American War. "Who is Philip II of Spain for whom our country was named?." 17 Feb. 2019, https://www.philstar.com/opinion/2019/02/17/1894312/who-philip-ii-spain-whom-our-country-was-named.

Philippines was part of the Spanish Empire as the Captaincy General of the Philippines for 333 years. Influences of Spain are apparent in Philippine culture, which are notable in the entire country. One of them is the Catholic faith. There were so many churches built during this period. In Bohol, we visited the Baclayon Church, which is actually the La Purisima Concepcion de la Virgen Maria Parish Church. The Baclayon Church was built in 1596 by the Jesuit priests. Interesting, too, was the museum, showcasing artifacts, books, icons, relics, and gold-stitched vestments. Augustinian Recollects succeeded the Jesuits in 1768, and heavily renovated the church since then ("Baclayon Church, *Wikipedia*, https://en.wikipedia.org/wiki/Baclayon_Church).

Our trip to the Philippines to celebrate the grand family reunion, my birthday, and Tony and my anniversary was well worth the expense and hassle. It could last forever and remain in the hearts of everyone. The feeling of excitement and the happiness of relatives and families assembled in that beautiful setting and event could not be measured in terms of money. It was the value of closeness and togetherness of families that mattered most. The money can be earned, but the time and opportunity may not come again.

This event left an imprint on immediate family members, cousins, and in-laws. It proved that a family gathering of this many could happen and succeed. Almost two hundred of us attended this grand family reunion.

Chapter 14
The Travel Buff in Me and Tony

The flyer stated, "Your Trip Includes:

- Roundtrip international airfare
- Transportation to and from JFK International Airport
- All domestic flights in China
- 4-and 5-star hotel accommodations
- 3 full meals each day
- Deluxe bus tour
- Fluent English-speaking tour guides
- Entrance fees for most attractions."

Who would want to miss this exciting mission trip to China by the Greater Bethesda-Chevy Chase Chamber of Commerce (now changed to the Greater Bethesda Chamber of Commerce)? Not Tony and I. Gloria Arnold of the chamber made the preparation for this trip smooth and easy. She obtained the visas to China, all the travel information, travel bag tags, name tags, conversion table using interbank exchange rate from US$ to Chinese yuan renminbi (CNY), and transportation to and from JFK. There were 32 chamber members and guests in the group.

On arriving in Beijing (Pi'kin in Mandarin, commonly as Peking), we were met by the local tour guide, who spoke excellent English and had a commanding personality. We were assigned to two big, modern motor coaches. Beijing, the sprawling capital city, was a total surprise. As of 2010, it was inhabited by over 19.6 million people as reported by the official Chinese Government Statistics Agency. It is a huge place with many, many tall buildings.

Before proceeding to our five-star hotel, Beijing Crowne Plaza Sun Palace, we had a feast of Peking roast duck. This fabulous restaurant was frequented by the late Mao Zedong, noted our guide. Accommodations were really the best. They were impeccably clean, and towels were new and fluffy.

Our third day was very busy. We visited the Temple of Heaven (built in AD 1420), viewed the 2008 Beijing Olympic venues such as the National Stadium, the Bird's Nest, and the Aquatic Center. On our way to visit the Great Wall, we stopped by a jade factory. Jade, which is usually green, is considered a lucky stone. It is known as the "stone of heaven." Jadeite is jade with a whitish shade and considered the most valuable of the jades. The Chinese have a saying that gold is valuable while jade is priceless. It symbolizes prosperity, success, good luck, and of renewal, longevity, as well as immortality.

The Great Wall of China is the most popular tourist destination in China. Who would not be amazed by this historical marvel of fortifications that is 13,171 miles long and 2,000 years old?

The Great Wall of China

The wall was built as protection from invaders. It was also used as an entry point to control trade and taxation, for cultural exchanges, control of immigration and emigration, and as a transportation corridor ("Great Wall of China," *Wikipedia*, https://en.wikipedia. org/wiki/Great_Wall_of_China). "How Long is the Great Wall of China? - WorldAtlas." 05 Dec. 2018, https://www.worldatlas.com/ articles/how-long-is-the-great-wall-of-china.html.

I walked over a mile of the wall. It was a very insignificant distance, but it's like acquiring bragging rights walking on this remarkable landmark.

Subsequent days were filled with educational and cultural insights of Chinese history. We visited the infamous Tiananmen Square. This was the site of the June 4, 1989, student protests calling for democracy, free speech, and free press in China. The demonstration ended with massacre of an estimated 2,700 to 3,400 people, though only about 300 were acknowledged ("1989 Tiananmen Square Protests and Massacre," *Wikipedia*, https://en.wikipedia.org/ wiki/1989_Tiananmen_Square_protests_and_massacre).

It should be noted that the fall of the Berlin Wall would occur a few months later, November 9, 1989. This was a time when countries in Central and Eastern Europe under socialist and communist regimes claimed their freedom and independence from the Soviet Union. When we asked our tour guide about the massacre and the tank man, he hushed-hushed and ignored us completely.

Next to visit and admire was the Palace Museum, also known as the Forbidden City. The Palace Museum is located in the Forbidden City, which is the museum itself. The Palace Museum was established in 1925, after the last emperor, Pu Yi, was evicted from the palace. *The Last Emperor*, a 1987 award-winning film, tells Pu Yi's story. It was filmed in the Forbidden City and captured the best visual features of this magnificent setting.

The Forbidden City was constructed from 1406 to 1420. It has 980 buildings and is built on 178 acres of land (7,750,016 square feet). With 9,999 rooms, it was the home of twenty-four emperors. The museum exhibits artifacts, paintings, calligraphy, ceramics, antiquities, porcelain, furniture, and many treasure troves left by China's emperors ("Forbidden City," *Wikipedia*, https://en.wikipedia.org/wiki/Forbidden_City). "How big is the Forbidden City? - China." 08 Apr. 2021, https://www.travelchinaguide.com/how-big-is-forbidden-city.htm.

We joined an optional tour of the hutongs to experience the living conditions and environment of ordinary Chinese people. Hutongs refer to the alleys formed by lines of courtyard residences that were traditional in northern Chinese cities like Beijing. A dozen of us joined the tour. We rode on rickshaws that were no longer pulled by the operator like a horse but by a pedicab, which was pedaled, not motorized. We went around the hutongs with houses lining these alleys. Some were wide, but most hutongs were narrow. People just hung around, playing, exercising, chatting, or just doing nothing. It was a community living style in which communal toilets and baths were common. There were stores, small establishments, and artists and vendors showing their crafts and just doing their business. The place was colorful with lanterns of red, green, and orange, and doors painted red.

We had lunch with a family living in one of the homes by the hutong. Traditional Chinese dishes were served, like rice, vegetables, and chicken. We met the owners, their daughter, and their granddaughter. We were told that their son was working in the United States.

We visited the usual tourist attractions, like the Summer Palace—with its long corridor gallery—Kumming Lake, Longevity Hill, the 17-Arch Bridge, and the Marble Boat. We were given free time to confer with local government people. I opted to visit the pearl market. I have learned that the gold sea pearl is more precious than the black sea pearl, and sea pearls are more valuable than cultured pearls. We were also introduced to cloisonne art, which is a decorative work in which enamel, glass, or gemstones are separated by strips of flattened wire placed edgewise on a metal backing. There were cloisonne jewelry, vases, figurines, knickknacks, and other decorative arts. At the auction company where I worked, I had often seen cloisonne consignments for auction.

Our early flight to Shanghai and motor coach ride to Suzhou went smoothly. Our local tour guide was clearly a product of China's one-child policy. The well-educated young woman was delightful with her exuberance and excitement. The Grand Canal boat ride was relaxing and a picturesque glimpse of waterside gardens, sacred landmarks, and people's dwellings. Some had laundry drying on lines outside.

This area is dubbed as "Venice of the East." I don't think so. I could have bypassed this excursion as there was nothing significant or exciting about it.

One thing our young tour guide told was that the concubines of the emperors were mostly from Suzhou. While in Shanghai girls spend an hour to do their faces, Suzhou girls took just thirty minutes. They were naturally beautiful.

It was in Hangzhou that we got to understand why mulberry trees are important in the silk industry. The mulberry leaves are the main food of the silkworms. The silkworms produce cocoons that are spun into silk thread. We had the opportunity to see how this was done. Then a visit to the National Embroidery Institute, where we saw the process of silk embroidery. It is so amazing and complicated. Of course, there was ample time to purchase silk bedsheets, pillows with silk cases, and scarves.

China is famous for tea. The best person to tell us about tea was none other than Dr. Tee. At Longjing Green Tea Plantation, we learned about planting, harvesting, and processing this aromatic and healthy beverage. The best tea, as was explained, is fresh, newly sprung, leaves of the tea plant. And the very best quality of them all are those picked in the springtime, compared to those picked at other times of the year. They command premium price. A pound of springtime green tea leaves then was $180, including a discount. Dr. Tee gave us lots of free tea but was undoubtedly also a great salesman.

I was not much impressed by Shanghai, although it is a very modern city with many skyscrapers, like New York City. We went to Shanghai's most popular place, the Bund (aka Waitan). It is less than a mile waterfront promenade along Huangpu River. It has about fifty-two buildings showcasing various architecture styles, including baroque, neoclassical, and gothic. They refer to it as a museum of buildings. I call it a copycat of iconic buildings in the West.

Shanghai's Magnetic Levitation Train (maglev) ride was an experience to remember. It is a commercial high-speed train cruising at 268 miles per hour. It is also the fastest commercial electric train in the world. We boarded the maglev at the Shanghai Pudong International Airport to Longyang Road Station and back. The distance between the two points is 18.6 miles, or 30 kilometers. At full speed, it takes seven minutes and twenty seconds to complete the two points ("Maglev Train," *Wikipedia*," https://en.wikipedia. org/wiki/Shanghai_maglev_train).

There was another maglev going opposite our direction, and we were advised to watch out for it. It was so fast that we did not know the trains had crossed. On our return, I posted my video camera by the window and waited for it. I got a shot of it that was not apparent at all, but I saw it as it is, as fast as a speeding bullet.

It is always interesting to notice the charm of every place we visited. I have seen the opulence and the hardship of life in both Beijing and Shanghai. Both have problems of pollution, traffic congestion, and swarms of street vendors. There were vendors of knockoffs and knockoffs of knockoffs. These terms were used by our tour guide to describe the fake, imitation, and counterfeit designer and luxury products like handbags, purses, and eyewear. Anyone interested can get them; just tell your tour guide. Some in our group went with our guide to a discreet location in a high-rise building and were happy to have purchased good imitation Louis Vuitton handbags—cheap. We were not allowed to buy food from street vendors or eat street food for our health and well-being while on this trip. The Chinese were health conscious, and everywhere there was space, people were exercising. It was mandated that everyone do an hour of exercise every day.

Joining an organized tour was very expedient, affordable, and with excellent accommodations. As for food, I am biased as I believe that Chinese food in the United States is better and with a higher quality of ingredients and condiments.

Living our lives now and not just hoping to live them after retirement, is just the best way for us. No matter how we look at it, considering all aspects of our lives' circumstances, there is no other way but to proceed as we envision. Retirement planning and savings are at the forefront, but they can wait for later.

Chapter 15
Victoria and Mercedes

We accumulated equity in our residential home. The application for refinance was approved, and we were allowed to withdraw funds to pay off debts with high monthly payments, like the auto loan, student loan, and high-interest credit cards. What a big relief. We consolidated our debts and were able to save a big chunk on high-interest loans. Most important, I learned great information from Charlie, our refinance processor. "Ludy, why don't you move to another house? Instead of paying too much in taxes to Uncle Sam, you can enjoy a bigger and nicer house with your current income."

I loved my house, my neighbors, and where I lived. It was just three miles from my office and so convenient. "But Charlie, if I did, how much of a house could I move to?"

"A million-dollar home."

"Are you sure?" I was incredulous.

"You and Tony have very good credit scores. You both have good qualifying incomes, and your debt-to-income ratios are good. Why not look into it?"

Charlie had seen it from one perspective, but I saw it from another. I was comfortable where we were and didn't want to move to a bigger house. It was just me and Tony now. The children were grown and didn't live with us anymore. We didn't need a bigger house, and we didn't want it. But the tax issue was a matter of concern too. If Charlie qualified us for a million-dollar home, we could qualify to buy a house between $400,000 and $500,000 without moving from our home. Wow! This was good. Thank you, Charlie, for this great idea. Let's see if it can be done.

I went astray from the plan when Johan showed me a historical Victorian home close to the County Government Center. There were new Victorian homes for sale in the area, and they were selling for a million to over a million dollars. But this registered historic house under consideration was one third lower in price than the new ones and better located. Even then, the price was unrealistically high for the amount for which we could readily get approved. But I had fallen in love with it.

I figured out where I would get the funds for down payment and the estimated monthly mortgage. I now planned to live in the Victorian home. I factored in the net rental income of our current home, my new salary adjustment as well as Tony's new rate. We got precertified loan approval. It was doable. We put in an offer and earnest money deposit. We visited the house several times. I liked it for its Victorian design, meaning that it was appreciated more for its form than its functionality. The Victorian had steep roofs, decorative gables, eaves, bay windows, high ceilings, and was painted in a variety of pastel blues, yellows, and greens. I was totally excited about it and imagined myself living in it.

The house required a lot of repairs, though. It had four levels, and the stairs were steep. Since it was old, the floors creaked, and the bathrooms had not been updated. The ceilings in the lower level were very low. The back door from the separate garage was so low that you had to bend to get in and out. I talked to the elderly couple living in a similar Victorian house next door. I inquired about the utility costs. They said they paid at least $400 per month for electricity alone. To save, they didn't turn on the air-conditioning system during summer; they just used the fan. They had lived there for about forty years.

I brought a friend and her husband over to get their feedback. It was not positive. I asked Johan his honest opinion. "This kind of home is not readily salable because they only appeal to certain types of people. For this reason, it has been on the market for quite a long time. You cannot make any renovations on the outside since they are historically protected. You have to get approval for any structural changes. Improvements and renovations inside the house can be made without approval." In short, Johan didn't recommend that we buy this house. He and Tony shared the same view. My friend was just like me. She loved the Victorian feel to it. I was already thinking of what home furnishings I would bid on from the auction house to make this home a Victorian home in its truest sense.

I passionately and persistently pursued it until Tony opened my eyes on the importance of being objective, not be emotional, in making the decision. I wondered, *At near retirement age, how long can we be strong enough to climb up four flights of stairs without falling and breaking our bones? How much will maintenance and upkeep of this huge house cost?*

Doubts had crept into the soundness of this intended buy. The good thing was that while we were negotiating the price, the sellers went on vacation and could not get back to us right away. They would counter our proposal, and we would then offer another counterproposal. At the end, we could not agree on a purchase price. The earnest money was returned, and I said goodbye to my dream of a Victorian home. I was emotionally engaged with the house, but my paradigm shift got the better hold of me.

At that time, I still had not changed much in my fancy lifestyle. I told myself that since I did not go home to Victoria, I deserved to take home a Mercedes. A brand-new iridium-silver 350 Mercedes Benz sedan was in our driveway soon after the Victorian episode. I justified it this way. By the time we retired, this car would be totally paid off. And it would still be a good car during our retirement years. We could drive it when visiting our Jewish-American-Filipino grandkid five hours northeast, and another seven hours northwest of Washington DC to visit the other set of Eurasian grandkids.

There were three cars parked at our garage and driveway for the two of us. We could not do away with the van since it could sit eight people. When our children and grandkids visited us, we could all get settled in this one vehicle. The Lexus was a spare for the Mercedes. That made sense to me. I did not think about insurance costs, maintenance costs, and registration fees. That was a mistake.

Chapter 16
Our Son's Marriage to a French Neuroscientist

Carl and his lovely girlfriend went to Paris, France, to visit her parents. There he asked for the father's permission to marry her. Carl charmed him with his knowledge of wines, cheeses, dogs, and many other things. Carl had varied interests and hobbies. He went from designing clothes to creating silk screen paintings, and raising and propagating poisonous Brazilian frogs; he cultured fruit flies as food for the frogs. Carl made a huge terrarium with exotic plants, raised varieties of orchids, and assembled computers and bikes. He built a computer for his sister's friend. It took him a year to finish because he lost interest in the middle of it. The friend had so much patience, and I wondered why. Eventually, he finished it after some pushing from his sister to get it done. By the way, the poisonous Brazilian frogs, especially the young poison dart frog, when taken out of its natural habitat, will lose toxicity. "8 Most Dangerous Frogs You Won't Dare to Keep - Reptiles' Cove." https://reptilescove.com/care/frogs/dangerous-frogs.

Carl went to Paris for the first time in 1996 as our graduation gift to him. Much later, he made another visit in connection with his job with a computer company. Then at the time when he went to put a platinum Cartier diamond ring on the finger of his sweetheart, who was from Paris. Carl took her to her favorite place, the Napoleon Bonaparte bridge Pont d'Iena. What makes the bridge astonishing is its location at the Eiffel Tower's feet. The structure was designed with five arches, each with an arc length of twenty-eight meters, and four intermediate piers. It was the perfect setting to propose as it offers a gorgeous view of one of the world's fascinating human engineering marvel the Eiffel Tower ("Pont d'Iéna," *Wikipedia*, https://en.wikipedia.org/wiki/Pont_d%27I%C3%A9na). "History of the Pont d'Iena bridge in Paris France - EUtouring." https://www.eutouring.com/pont_d_iena_history.html.

It was a year-long engagement. It gave me a year to set aside funds for the wedding. I was very happy that my son was getting married at age thirty-four. They planned to hold it at a place in Du Pont Circle in Washington DC for their closest friends and family. When I told him how much we would contribute financially, he totally turned around and made a great wedding plan.

The ceremony was arranged to take place October 15, 2011, at the International Trade Center in the Horizon Room. Cocktails and the reception would be held at the Rotunda, at 1300 Pennsylvania Ave. It was near the Willard Intercontinental DC, which was the wedding party's hub and some international guests were billeted.

The Rotunda at the International Trade Center

The International Trade Center is the first and only federal building dedicated to serve both government and private establishments. Guests were advised to bring passports or IDs to enter the building. After the wedding ceremony, guests could get to the reception by elevator. It was easy and convenient for everyone. From the Rotunda, you could view the White House on the northwest of Pennsylvania Ave., and the US Capitol on the southwest.

It was an early autumn evening, and the air was crisp. The usual hot, humid, and hazy forecast in Washington was absent. The bride was beautiful and radiant in her very special wedding gown. Her bridesmaids wore bluish-gray gowns that made them look like pretty fairies. Not to be outdone, the groom looked dashing in his tailored suit. The groomsmen looked sharp and handsome.

I was very impressed by the wedding planner, who was on top of everything down to the littlest detail. There was an open bar with exquisite wines and hot and cold hors d'oeuvres. The first course was sauteed wild mushrooms forestiere with creamy polenta. The entrée consisted of tenderloin of beef and lobster tail, a melange of vegetables, and sundried tomato risotto cake. And for dessert, pinot noir poached winter fruit pavlova. The wedding cake was a macaron tower of various flavors.

The program was spontaneous and fun with and lots of dancing and a variety of music to accommodate the baby boomers and the Generation Xers. The party was lively. I had my selected guests, which included Abdi and Simin Parvizian, Stephanie Kenyon and Randy Beehler, and Andrea Roane and Mike Skehan.

The guests came from California, New York, Washington, Virginia, Maryland, Pennsylvania, New Jersey, North Carolina, Wisconsin, Nevada, Philippines, France, Spain, Switzerland, Austria, and Germany. The wedding was especially graced by the bride's grandmother, who came from France, and Carl's grandmother and great-aunt from California.

I believed that what begins well most likely will end well. This was one of the motivations that made me take action to straighten up our financial mess. It feels so good when we have the freedom to spend and enjoy life without charging them to credit cards or other sources.

I was very pleased and proud that we were halfway through our obligation. One more wedding to go.

Chapter 17
A Crash Course in Financial Education

Tony and I were now psychologically ready to face squarely the matter of retirement funding. To retire successfully in due time had long been in the forefront of the plan, but it was always pushed back for a life of ease and present convenience. Preference was definitely for instant gratification and indulgence and not self-sacrifice. This was when self-discipline was especially required to succeed. It was, however, still wanting.

According to Wallethub.com, to ensure a comfortable life in one's elderly years, one should be debt-free by age forty-five so you can ramp up retirement savings. An average American consumer has about $25,483 debt aside from a mortgage. An average American homeowner carries a mortgage balance of $215,655 ("Experian: Americans Are Maintaining Healthy Credit," October 20, 2020," https://www.pressreleasepoint.com/experian-americans-are-maint aining-healthy-credit-profiles-during-covid-19-pandemic). Tony and I were way beyond the suggested debt-free age. We had debts in the hundreds of thousands and nominal savings. It had become very scary to look at our financial position of negative net worth.

When asked by CNBC Select, Faron Daugs, CFP and CEO of Harrison Wallace Financial Group, stated the following ten habits of self-made millionaires:

1. They avoid debt.
2. They buy their cars, and plan to keep them long-term.

3. They have emergency funds.
4. They invest.
5. They take advantage of everything their employer has to offer.
6. They don't try to keep up with the Joneses.
7. They utilize tax deductions.
8. They look for other income streams—passive income/rental income.
9. They start saving for their kids' college early on.
10. They seek advice.

("10 Money Habits of Self-Made Millionaires," CNBC, https://www.cnbc.com/select/money-habits-of-self-made-millionaires/).

Could Tony and I become millionaires? Let's see:

1. Fail: We sought, not avoided debt.
2. Pass: We bought brand-new cars and kept them long term.
3. Fail: None at the time, but we agreed we should start an emergency fund.
4. Fail: We had none but thought we should start to invest.
5. Fail: My employer offered none of that, but Tony's did.
6. Fail: Well, we didn't try to act *like* the Joneses, we thought and acted like we *were* the Joneses, but without the means and relying on credit resources.
7. Pass: We contributed to IRAs and a 401k to minimize payment of federal and state income taxes. Mortgage interest and property tax payments on our home were tax deductions.
8. Fail: We had no such streams at the time, but we knew it would be good to consider earning passive income immediately.
9. Fail: It was too late to save for college, so we resorted to Sallie Mae educational loans.
10. Pass: We were seeking advice, attended seminars, and read books on finances.

We only passed three out of ten. How could we improve our batting average to make our dreams happen? Let us look at the seven habits we failed.

#1: Avoiding debt is good. We resolved to cut down on costs, earn more, live within our means, and save. This required a lot of self-discipline and hardcore adjustments in our lifestyle. But this was a reality we needed to face immediately. There would be no retirement in sight without this first step.

#3: It is suggested that a reserved fund for emergencies be about three to six times one's monthly income. This fund can be tapped in for things such as major auto repair, medical emergency, or to provide for living expenses in case of layoff or between jobs. It helps prevent increasing credit card debt.

#4: We needed to invest in the right program for our needs and circumstances. I wasn't very comfortable in investing in stocks, but I learned there were options to build wealth outside the stock market.

#5: With the salary I received from my employer, I saved on my own, if ever. Tony took advantage of benefits the state offered by contributing to his 401(k) and 401(a) to the maximum that is matched by the state.

#6: Lack of personal self-discipline is the number 1 difference between the rich, the poor and the middle class, this according to Robert Kiyosaki in *Rich Dad Poor Dad*. It is this lack of self-discipline that causes people who get a raise to immediately go out and buy a new car or take a cruise. I am not just living up to the Joneses. I am Mrs. Jones. I need to stop thinking and acting that I am Mrs. Jones.

#8: True, passive income, like residual income from earned insurance premiums, interest earned from investments and rental income from realty investments is exciting to have. These are earnings earned not by work but by money working for me.

#9: *Money*'s cover story in its "101 Ways to Build Wealth," recommends to those between the ages of thirty-five and forty-four to fund a 529. This allows money saved for tuition bills to grow tax-free "Ways to Build Wealth," CNN, https://money.cnn.com/magazines/moneymag/101-ways-build-wealth/.

In our case, it was too late. But we believed in investing in education. Robert Kiyosaki said to invest first in education. And in reality, the only real asset we have are our minds, and it is the most powerful tool we have dominion over. According to "101 Ways to Build Wealth," it stated in number 59 that those Aged 45–54, the Peak Earning Years, is to go easy on the school loans. Saying no to your kid is hard, which may explain why parent PLUS loan balances have doubled over the past ten years. But taking out lots of those loans, which carry a 7.9 percent rate, can be risky. "If you have to resort to PLUS loans to pay for college, it's probably a sign you can't afford the college," says Kantrowitz. A good rule of thumb: Don't borrow more than you can repay within ten years or by retirement, whichever is first ("101 Ways to Build Wealth") CNN. https://money.cnn.com/magazines/moneymag/101-ways-build-wealth/.

Our educational loans were partly paid on a monthly installment for several years and fully paid in January 2009, which was within the time frame set by Kantrowitz. Should I have saved that in my retirement account? Should I have deprived my child of the opportunity to go to college so I could retire comfortably? Did I have the heart to tell her that we cannot afford her college costs? Definitely not. Instead of looking at the problem, we looked for solutions. Incurring a debt to educate our child was well thought of. Education of children was an investment that would pay back many times fold. It produces intergenerational and multigenerational benefits and advancements.

The reward of that sacrifice for the betterment of the next generation was immeasurable. What if we hadn't? What could have happened? We knew that she would certainly do whatever it took to achieve her goals. I can't imagine the hardship that our daughter would have gone through had we not taken the action.

Chapter 18
Good Breaks and Good Decisions

The S & P 500 price dropped in 2000 due to the crash of the dot-com bubble. It took eight years to recover, and that was immediately followed by the crash of 2008. It took about six years for prices to recover to their previous all-time highs ("Here's How Long the Stock Market Has, *Four Pillar Freedom,* June 21, 2018, https://fourpillarfreedom.com/heres-how-long-the-stock-market-has-historically-taken-to-recover-from-drops/).

Before the recession, Tony and I were in a position to face our situation head-on. We already had the facts and were ready to face the reality of our financial dilemma. We had to address our debt problems, change our lifestyle, and focus on our retirement issue. We decided to do the following:

1. Refinance to a lower mortgage interest rate, pay off debts, and start an emergency fund.

    To consolidate the high-interest revolving credits to a low interest regular monthly installment, it was necessary to refinance our mortgage loan. In ten years, the appraised value of our home had increased to three times of our purchase price. We refinanced it at a low interest rate of 6.25 percent and paid off the HELOC balance of $87,982. As always, our credit ratings were very high. We were dedicated to our jobs and working hard to progress and get promotions.

    During the economic crash in 2008, interest rates

plummeted. We took the opportunity to refinance again, this time from 6.25 percent to 4.875 percent, which reduced our monthly mortgage payment. In addition, we cashed out $47,289.75 from our equity and paid our credit card debts. We paid off the Lexus, and made partial payments on Sallie Mae and to Home Depot for the home improvements. Since we were paying less monthly mortgage, we were able to set aside some funds for an emergency.

2. We decided to invest in real estate since interest rates were low, and there were distressed home sales. The purchase of the property that I co-owned with my sister was done during the recession period. The interest rate was at 5.5 percent. Two years later, we refinanced it at the rate of 3.875 percent.

3. We bought big items that were sold at bargain prices during the recession. About this time, we did some home improvements, like renovating the kitchen, installing new appliances and marble countertops, and constructing a better front porch and driveway. The cost of these renovations were funded by what we saved from the reduced monthly mortgage. And the purchase of materials were at bargain prices.

4. Other ways to live and move on during the recession included cutting back on expenses and living within our means. This was challenging indeed. There were already big-expense items in the pipeline. We had to cut those we could, but for those to which we were committed, we had to go through with the purchases and cover them in some way later.

We have a few more things to work on to be credit card free. But it has felt good to make great strides toward achieving our goals. We maintained our philosophy to live the life we love and love the life we live. This made us strong and kept us going through the challenges that faced us every day.

There had to be something we can do to augment our income to pay off our debts and be ready to set aside funds for our retirement. We were just a few more years before reaching full-benefit retirement age. We knew we should do something now to get to where we want to be, that is, to retire without worrying where to get funding for our living expenses, medical care, and cost of travel and lifestyle amenities.

Chapter 19

Project Retirement Income Source: Third Purchase

Charlie planted the idea in my brains when he encouraged me to pursue the purchase of another property. Based on his advice, it assured Tony and me that we were still good for approval of another mortgage. I checked with Johan if he had something to show us that would meet the criteria we are looking for. He had a rambler style in a fine neighborhood. It looked impressive on the outside, but inside, it was dirty and unkempt, and it needed a lot of repairs and refurbishments. When I asked him why he brought us there, Johan said, "This is a short sale. You see no for sale sign for sale in front of the house."

He showed me a similar house along Flora Lane, just three houses down, that was on the market. I checked it out. It was being offered for over $130,000 more than the short-sale house. Even if we spent $50,000 to update the rambler, we would surely still be ahead. "The bank's asking price is low compared to the other house because banks are not in house-selling business," Johan explained. "The bank's purpose is to liquidate their real estate inventory, turn them to cash, and collect what is owed to the bank. The problem in this short-sale transaction is that the bank can wait for months before responding to the offer because they are also waiting for other offers."

I decided to make an offer in the amount equivalent to the

bank's asking price. After two months, the bank countered with an offer of $120,000 above their original asking price. They probably knew the price of the other house for sale in the neighborhood. With the new stated price, I would rather buy the other house on the market, which was ready for occupancy. "No, my offer stays," I replied. After another two months, I received an adjusted offer of $100,000 lower than the second asking price. I was almost tempted to agree, but I thought, *There is no other party interested in the house. I have no competitor. Why compete and outbid myself?* I told them my offer stood.

While the bank was taking its time to decide about my final offer, I started to check out where I could source the funds to buy the short-sale property. How could we possibly fund the purchase of a third single-family home? Tony and I decided to tap into our IRA funds, take the cash value of our variable annuity insurance, and our savings. The consequence of this move was that we would pay a 10 percent penalty for early withdrawal and the corresponding income tax on retirement funds and interest on the cash value loan. The hard part was that we would only receive the cash value of the annuities, not its accumulated annuity value. One of the accounts, my IRA, had an accumulated value of $32,445.19. We would receive just $27,760, which was net of 14.44 percent. This was stiff. Why pay a penalty when I withdraw to use my own money? It is just the way it works. On the other hand, this purchase was a bargain if we succeeded in our bid. It was an exchange of IRA in the stock market to real estate investment. We thought we were getting a great deal in this exchange anyway.

The bank came up with their response after maybe two or three weeks, and closing was set. I was glad I had been patient and weighed all the important aspects of the transaction. We bought it at the original offered price, $110,000 less than the house down the street. Repairs and renovations took place immediately, using the excess funds from closing. The house was an ugly duckling when I first saw it. Grease all over the kitchen, the floors were scratched, the bathrooms were dirty, the tubs and faucets did not work, drawers didn't close, the fireplace was dirty with soot and ashes. And the air-conditioning, heater, range, and washer and dryer needed replacement. A total makeover, and renovations were finished.

I had a reliable contractor who had done repairs and improvements at our residence before. He willingly agreed to work with us immediately. When finished, the ugly duckling turned out to be a sleek and beautiful swan. In over a month, Johan placed it on the market for rental. It was leased for two years to respectable tenants. The rental income was more than double the monthly amortization we pay on the property.

At this juncture, Tony and I were now using other people's money to acquire assets and accumulate income for my retirement. I was happy that I made the right decision of turning my back to the Victorian house. *Would it be okay to rent out two bedrooms of the main house or the basement with a bedroom and separate kitchen of the Victorian home to strangers so we can recoup some of the maintenance costs and help lower our mortgage payments?* Those were some of the crazy ideas that came to my mind to justify the acquisition of that dream house. It was not meant to be. I pass by that ex-future Victorian home of mine every now and then. I feel happy when I see it because better opportunities, like this third purchase, surfaced to help fulfill our desire to retire comfortably.

As a mom-and-pop landlord, this has not always been easy. Tony and I attended to the tenants' complaints about leaking faucets to noisy air conditioners, water not heating enough, front porch railing wiggling, clogged garbage disposal, sump pump that did not work, flooded lower level, rats, and many more. Some tenants call 24/7 for the littlest concern that they could handle themselves. Most of the tenants, though, were gracious and polite, and they understood the importance of good relationships. These services could be taken care of by a property manager, but that would take a good part of the income. To endure this pain and suffering was necessary to achieve gain.

I was exposed to ownership of real estate at a very tender age. Families on my mother's side own tracts of farmland planted with rice, coconuts, and sugarcane. My parents always owned a sizable residential lot on which sits our family home built for our big family. They also went into buying and selling rice land and land planted with avocados, jackfruit, vegetables, and mango trees. Rice land farming was hardly profitable, the Philippines being in the typhoon belt section of the world.

As for me and Tony, we purchased our first home six months after our marriage. The proceeds from the sale of that house provided the down payment for our first home in the United States. I have always had a close attachment to land and real estate ownership. At twenty-five, I had already purchased a piece of property in a subdivision in metro Manila that I paid on a monthly installment plan. As far as I was concerned, it was in real estate where I could be comfortable putting my hard-earned money for safekeeping and growth. Fortunately, I was both lucky and blessed most of the time and was able to purchase the properties at reasonable prices during a buyers' market. Moreover, they were located in a desirable area with a good school district, accessibility, and in a good neighborhood. I realized it to be true that in real estate, the rule is location, location, location.

When I asked advice from Manoucher Parvizian, Abdi's older brother, about a property I was considering buying, he told me, "Location is the key. Even if the house is not that great looking for it is what you can afford, at least it has to be in a good location and good neighborhood."

And a friend who was an architect told me, "Buy a house that is built with good construction materials. The plumbing and electrical fixtures can be repaired and replaced, but the structure, foundation, and construction materials are critical for a house to be considered good."

This third purchase is our passive income source for now. The rental was more than twice the monthly mortgage payments. At last, we have this as an additional source of retirement income. We're using other people's money to build our assets. This purchase was funded by cashing out our IRAs, where we lost a lot on penalties for early withdrawal from the government and from the insurance company. This experience made me realize that the financial vehicle we used to accumulate funds for our retirement was not the appropriate one. We found a better avenue.

Chapter 20
A Critical Time: Is It?

Three years before reaching my full retirement age, Tony and I agreed to retire at the same time. He would extend his employment by one year so that by then, I would have reached my full retirement age. We have three outstanding mortgages: our residence, my joint tenancy with my sister, and the rental.

In addition to the three mortgages, we still had debts to be paid:

1.	Sallie Mae for student loan	$43,000
2.	Mercedes Benz	$42,782
3.	Home Depot	$5,700
4.	Various credit cards	$10,070

Our bank granted us an HELOC for $110,000 at an interest rate of 3.99 percent. We decided to pay off the Sallie Mae loan with a 5.8 percent interest rate. The auto loan was paid monthly with interest at 2.99 percent. We decided it was better to keep it as is because it would be fully paid before our retirements. Home Depot was a no-interest account but had to be paid within the specified period. This debt was already included in our monthly budget. The various credit card debts were now just a fraction of our regular balances. We figured out that within a year, they will all be paid off. From this point on, we will still use the credit cards but pay them in full each month and leave no balance.

On retirement, we planned that the mortgage on our residence would be budgeted from our monthly income: Tony's Social Security and state pension and my Social Security. The joint tenancy will be under my sister Agnes's account, with me as support if needed. The Flora Lane rental house pays for itself and gives my retirement income boost. Finally, the HELOC debt was paid in full in two years. The critical time—retirement—was at hand, and we were facing it squarely. What a feeling of relief knowing that there was a solution to our financial mess.

Chapter 21

Three Years to Go: 2013—a Year of Birth, Death, and a River Cruise

A milestone in our life happened during this period. We became grandparents for the first time when Anais Lourdes was born in Lucile Packard Children's Hospital in Stanford, Palo Alto, California. Carl and Laurence lived in California, where Laurence work as a neuroscientist at Stanford University, and Carl was a computer architect for AT&T. Anais was so adorable even at birth. Being a Eurasian could be one reason for it.

At this same time, my mother got sick and was hospitalized in Los Angeles. Tony and I cut short our visit with Anais in Palo Alto and flew down to be with my gravely ill mother. All my siblings came to be with her. We decided to bring her to Silver Spring, Maryland, to live with my sister, Agnes. She was taken to Holy Cross Hospital in Silver Spring to reassess her medical condition. In less than a month, we were advised to put her under full-time medical care. We arranged for her stay in a nursing home rehab in Chevy Chase, which is very close to where we live. We took turns checking her condition and coordinating with medical personnel. This reminded me of an incident that happened seventeen years before, when my father was confined in another nursing home rehab in Chevy Chase. He sustained a severe head injury when he was bumped by a vehicle.

Long before my mother's illness, Tony and I arranged to go on a river cruise. We planned to cancel it, but when I told her, she would not hear of it. "Just go live your life," she said in her weak voice.

I hugged her and said, "Wait for me and Tony to come back. Don't leave us yet. Be strong."

We went on an eight-day Viking River Cruise dubbed the Rhine Getaway. After the cruise, we would spend three days in Amsterdam, The Netherlands. When traveling, I always want to know the history and significance of the place visited. Travel, to me, is experiencing in person the stories, news, and pictures seen in print and on television. We boarded the longship *Viking Atla*, the name of a Norse goddess of water. The Viking explorers had their heydays from the eighth to the eleventh centuries. They were known for their ship-building ingenuity and technology, particularly their innovated longships. They were able to maneuver along rivers and oceans, establishing trading settlements and spreading their Scandinavian culture in various areas in Europe, Russia, Greenland, and many other places.

We were met at the airport and transferred to the *Viking Atla*.

Viking Atla docked in Basel, Switzerland

What a thrill it was to experience our first European river cruise. We started cruising on the Rhine River, starting from Basel, Switzerland. Marianne van Hoogdalen, our program director, was from the Netherlands. She provided us with *Viking Daily,* a history of the place we were visiting on that day. Basel is a quintessential gateway city. It is in Switzerland but adjacent to both Germany and France and is divided in half by the Rhine River. It is close to the Jura Mountains, which demarcate the French and Swiss border, and the Black Forest, a mountainous region of southwest Germany that borders France. Basel is just over an hour's drive from Lucerne and Zurich in Switzerland, and one and a half hours from the Strasbourg Alsace region of France. It is a major industrial center for banking and for chemical and pharmaceutical industries. It has more than three dozen museums, from art and architecture to cartoons and dollhouses. In 1225, this cosmopolitan city was first to construct a bridge across the Rhine. It established Switzerland's first university, the University of Basel, in 1460.

A dinner in a huge restaurant that accommodated all the guests culminated our first day on board the ship. The food was scrumptious and the service impeccable. Before dessert was served, Aleksander Jovic, the maître d', came out with a special cake for Tony. It was a milestone, his sixty-fifth birthday. It was truly memorably special and very touching. When we got to our veranda suite, there was a personal birthday note from the crew for Tony.

Viking Atla cruised the Rhine as we slept restfully in a very comfortable accommodation. When we awoke, we were in Breisach, Germany. We went on an excursion to Germany's famous Black Forest. The Black Forest is called that because it is a very dense forest of pine and fir trees, and the ground underneath could barely see the sun. We watched a cuckoo clock-making workshop and, of course, listened to the sales pitch. There are still traditional mechanically operated cuckoo clocks, but many are battery operated. The wood used in the clocks come from the pine trees of the forest. Yes, a cuckoo bird comes out the window of the clock and sounds the number of hours of the time. We had a Black Forest cake at the Black Forest, including a demonstration of how it was made. What we visited was just a teeny part of what the Black Forest offers. Maybe we'll continue the visit at some other time. In the afternoon, we joined an optional tour of Colmar, a quaint town in the Alsace region of France.

Back at the *Atla* on this second day, we had a welcome cocktail at the lounge and a welcome dinner at the restaurant, where we had the chance to meet the staff and fellow guests.

Atla docked at the German town of Kehl. We boarded a motor coach that took us across the Rhine to Strasbourg in France. Strasbourg was founded by the Romans in 12 BC. It became independent in 1262, but in 1681, it became part of France. In 1870, Germany invaded it, and at the end of World War 1, in 1918, France reclaimed Strasbourg. Today, it is the capital of the Alsace region. Strasbourg is a center of European politics, home to the European Council and the European Parliament, which meets at the Palais de L' Europe, and the European Council of Human Rights. Strasbourg also has the distinction of being the first city in the world whose historic center, the Grand Ile—with twenty-one bridges that connects it to the rest of the city—has been classified entirely as a UNESCO World Heritage Site. It is also famous for its sandstone Gothic cathedral, whose construction started in 1176 and completed nearly three hundred years later. An astronomical clock was added in the fourteenth century.

We were excited to join the excursion to Heidelberg. It is the home of Heidelberg University. Established in 1386, it is the oldest university in Germany. Heidelberg was a hub of artists, writers and scholars from all over the world. It inspired Johann Wolfgang von Goethe's poetry and J. M. W. Turner's landscapes. Mark Twain— Samuel Langhorne Clemens—found inspiration there for his second travel book, *A Tramp Abroad.*

Heidelberg is known to Tony and me and is close to our hearts. It was at Alte University (Old Heidelberg University) that Jose Rizal, a student then but who later became a national hero of the Philippines, studied ophthalmology in 1886. It was there that he wrote a poem, "A Las Flores de Heidelberg" ("To the Flowers of Heidelberg"). He lived in a nearby town, Wilhelmsfeld for about three months, where he wrote the final chapters of his book, *Noli Me Tangere* (*Touch Me Not*), which was published in Berlin in 1887. This book, and *El Filibusterismo* (*The Reign of Greed*), which was published in 1891, angered both the Spanish colonial elite and many educated Filipinos due to their symbolism. These books resulted in Rizal's being prosecuted as the inciter of the Philippine revolution against Spain. He was tried by the military, convicted and executed by firing squad by the Spaniards on December 30, 1896. The Philippines declared its independence from Spain on June 12, 1898 ("Dr. Jose P. Rizal, 1861–1896," *Discover Philippines*, https://sites.google.com/site/discoverphilippineswithus/dr-jose-p-rizal).

Heidelberg castle is a must-see structure in Germany. The castle that took four hundred years to build was not spared from damage during the Thirty Years' War that took place in 1618 to 1648. This war was a 17th-century religious conflict fought primarily in central Europe. It remains one of the longest and most brutal war in human history, with more than eight million casualties resulting from military battles as well as from the famine and disease caused by the conflict. "Thirty Years' War - HISTORY." 09 Nov. 2009, https://www.history.com/topics/reformation/thirty-years-war.

Rebuilding of the Heidelberg castle began immediately each time, but reconstruction was never completed. In 1764, still in the rebuilding phase lightning caused a major fire and destruction. "Heidelberg Castle Facts - Explore romantic Schloss Heidelberg in Germany." https://www.germany-insider-facts.com/heidelberg-castle.html. It remains to be a magnificent castle ruins worth visiting.

The bombs of World War II spared Heidelberg, thus

preserving its Baroque charm, historic churches, and castle. While many German cities faced severe destruction during the Second World War, Heidelberg was largely spared by the allied bombings. Historians presume that firstly the city wasn't seen as strategically important and secondly that the US had already eyed on establishing a garrison here after the end of the war. "10 Facts About Heidelberg You Need to Know - Culture Trip." 16 Dec. 2017, https://theculturetrip.com/europe/germany/articles/10-facts-about-heidelberg-you-need-to-know/.

The middle Rhine, between Koblenz and Bingen in Germany, has been listed as a UNESCO World Heritage Site since 2002. Cruising the Rhine and passing through its scenic views was like watching a movie. There were many centuries-old castles, palaces, and fortresses along this stretch. This section is a paradise for those who are enthusiasts of architectural design. I could see from afar and enjoyed the vista, but it was not complete. I didn't feel or experience being a part of the place. I found it wanting, and I craved more.

Of the many castles we passed along the Rhine, we visited the Marksburg Castle. It was set high on the peak of a hilltop overlooking the Rhine Valley and the city of Braubach. The motor coach took us up to the hill. The view below and around it was spectacular. Walking over cobblestones, steps, and uneven ground was a challenge. I made sure to wear a sturdy pair of shoes that protected my ankles from spraining or hurting my plantar fascia. The German Association of Castles' headquarters is in Marksburg Castle.

Cologne is dominated by its Catholic cathedral, the Kolner Dom, or The Dom. Of Gothic architectural design, it has filigreed twin spires that shoot up the skyline of Cologne. One of the places I spent time was the Fragrance Museum Farina House, which claims to be the birthplace of eau de Cologne. I am familiar with the fragrance as it was like my father's cologne. I could have gotten him his favorite cologne, but I was fifteen years late. I thought this would be a good present for friends and family in the United States. It was also on sale.

Cologne is also known for its German delicacy of pork knuckles and famous Kolsch beer. We joined the optional visit to the Brauhaus, a café that serves Kolsch beer. Our local guide took us to several beerhouses for beer tasting, such as Peters Brauhaus Kolsch, Paffgen Kolsch (established in 1883), Brauhaus Sunner im Walfisch and Colner Hofbrau Frau. The Brauhaus zur Malzmuehle, established in 1858, had photos of President Bill Clinton enjoying his Muhlen Kolsch. These beerhouses were filled with locals and adventurous people like us.

Kinderdijk, Netherlands, has the largest concentration of operational windmills. Cited as a UNESCO World Heritage Site in 1997, these windmills have powerful mill sails for catching the wind and turn large paddlewheels that scoop water from the polders. This is one way of reclaiming land. The wind sails have now been taken over by modern pumping stations, which was what we saw at the entrance of the venue. We went inside a small museum for an orientation about the operation of the windmills and were shown the principles of hydro-management at the site. The tour of the interior of a working windmill showed us that it was the cramped living quarters of a family. They were required to maintain the windmill in working condition. It was raining so hard and cold as we walked around the dikes while listening to the stories and information relayed continuously by the expert.

Cruising was a pleasurable way to travel. No packing and unpacking except on the first and last days. Every day there was time and opportunities to learn about many topics, including cooking regional specialties, coffee making, a talk about the European Union by a guest lecturer, glassblowing demonstration, talk about and tasting delicious Dutch cheeses and how to navigate Europe's rivers. One could join in on any of the scheduled activities, enjoy cocktails and live music in the lounge, go to the Aquavit for bar snacks and an after-dinner drink, or listen to music and dance in the lounge. There was always a daily briefing for the next day's excursions and events.

Our program director, Marianne, spoke several languages and was very entertaining. She sometimes wore costumes and rendered some songs from the old days.

Marianne and me in costumes

Marianne called us by our first names and even remembered a little bit of our personal information, which was endearing. Marianne was very informative about the views along the river and the confluence of different rivers into the Rhine. There could be a problem when the rivers had different water levels. We had an incident about it, but ours was operated by the Vikings and we got through it as expected.

At the captain's farewell dinner, we bade goodbye to our newly found friends with the hope of meeting again. I have maintained occasional communications with Laura and Bill Cowser since we met eight years ago.

At 2 a.m., *Atla* arrived in Amsterdam and at 9 a.m., everyone was ready to disembark and proceed to the airport for flights home. At the time of booking, we had already arranged to take the post-cruise extension for three days.

While cruising to Amsterdam, I received a phone call from Agnes. She was crying uncontrollably. Then in a weak voice, she said, "Nanay [Mother] has left us." I could still hear her sobbing, and I imagined the grief on her face. A big pang hit me; I felt numb. I didn't seem to know what to do. And I felt sorry I went through with the cruise. I just remembered my mother was the leader in our family, with my father as the support. Raising ten children and taking them to where they are today was indeed an amazing achievement.

I offered a fervent prayer for her soul to rest in peace. "She could not wait for us to be back," I said. I felt extreme disappointment and much sorrow. She was gone for eternity, and I was not at her bedside to kiss her goodbye. But then I remembered what she said to me: "Just go live your life."

Tony and I couldn't change our schedule. We decided to finish our visit in Amsterdam. A Viking host was available and very helpful in planning our itinerary, so we made the most of our visit. First on our list was a visit to Rijksmuseum, where one can discover Dutch culture and history. The Rijksmuseum was established in 1798. It has an enormous exhibition space of approximately 129,168 square feet spread over a four-story building. Only about eight thousand out of its million artworks are displayed at a time. During our visit in 2013, its exhibits consisted of arts and history, crafts, art nouveau from special collection and art from 1100 to 2000.

Possibly the most famous is *The Night Watch* (1642) by Rembrandt van Rijn. It shows the officers and other militiamen of District II in Amsterdam. The painting shows seventeen militiamen who paid on average, 100 guilders each, a comfortable amount, depending on their place in the painting. Rembrandt painted sixteen other figures to create a dynamic effect. A number of people were viewing this masterpiece during our visit. "The Night Watch - Wikipedia." https://en.wikipedia.org/wiki/The_Night_Watch. "Who Commissioned Rembrandt To Paint The Night Watch?." 11 Jun. 2022, https://www.forthepeoplecollective.org/who-commissioned-rembrandt-to-paint-the-night-watch/.

The Netherlands, or Amsterdam, is often associated with tulips. *Still Life with Flowers* (1639), by Hans Bollongier, was prominently displayed. I was immensely attracted to it. The tulips that were the main focal point of the painting were the Semper Augustus, a rare variety of tulips. Red flame-like strokes were streaked on white bulb. One bulb was reportedly sold for 6,000 guilders. This price could have bought a house in Herengracht, one of the most prestigious addresses by the ring of canals. It was said that Bollongier did not paint this from life since there were seven of these dearest tulips in the painting.

I learned that Vincent can Gogh, who was then still an unknown painter, was the first visitor of the Rijksmuseum in October 1885. He was an admirer of Rembrandt. A self-portrait of van Gogh in 1887 is exhibited in the gallery.

The Milkmaid (1660), by Johannes Vermeer, is another outstanding work. She was not really a milkmaid but a housemaid. It is called such probably because the most amazing feature of the painting, the milk being poured out of the pitcher, actually appears to be flowing.

The Netherlands is one of the few countries in the world where prostitution is legalized. There has to be something regarding this subject in art. One was a 1720 drawing by Cornelis Troost titled, *Prince Eugene of Savoy in the Brothel of Mm Traese in the Prinsengracht with a Parade of Prostitutes.* The drawing shows the parading women with their skirts lifted, showing their bottoms. The prince seems to enjoy it, but could not decide which one to pick (https://www.amazon.com/Discover-Amsterdam-Rijksmuseum-short-walks/dp/9059373545).

Moving around Amsterdam was easy by foot, bicycle or boat. The next place we had to see was the house where Anne Frank, her family and others hid in the secret annex. There she wrote the diary that became an international bestseller and translated into more than fifty languages. Anne Frank was one of the million victims of the Nazi persecution of the Jews during World War II. The hiding place was the back house of the company building; eight people lived there in hiding for two years. The door to the annex was concealed by a movable bookcase that was especially made to hide the entrance. Opaque glassine paper covered the windows on the landing, preventing it from being seen from the front house. Anne Frank's story did not end well. They were arrested by the Nazis and brought to concentration camps. Anne Frank died in February 1945, in Bergen-Belsen concentration camp from typhus, exhaustion, lack of food, and horrible living conditions. It might have ended differently had she lived two more months as the camp was liberated on April 15, 1945 (*Anne Frank's House: A Museum with a Story,* English museum guide).

Amsterdam is referred to as the Venice of the North for its rings of canals. We took an Amsterdam canal cruise that allowed us to see various places around the city. There were boat houses on the canals that were inhabited; some were for rent. It was a very different lifestyle. I liked the relaxed environment and the easy way of life. Along the canal were historical buildings, churches, and many interesting architectural structures.

Amsterdam canal boat houses

Afterward, we joined a tour led by a local guide. Just like in our previous travels, we learned many facets of the place through these knowledgeable local tour guides. He took us to an area where coffee shops do not serve coffee but cannabis. These are cannabis stores. You can get the weed, hash, marijuana that you like.

Now that we had learned more about Amsterdam, we felt confident to explore on our own. Our curiosity led us to the red-light district at De Wallen. At first I didn't realize that we were right there. To my astonishment, I saw a gorgeous woman, almost totally naked, in a glass window on the other side of the road. Then I looked over to the side where I was walking and in another glass window was an equally beautiful almost naked woman. There was a window without a woman. I learned she might be busy with a customer. In almost every glass window was woman standing there, barely wearing anything at all. Almost all the women I saw were stunning, voluptuous, pretty, and seductive. It was not proper to stare or take pictures of these sex workers. They were independent workers who paid income taxes. And they had to be licensed before engaging in their work.

We strolled along the corridor of glass windows as women offered their prostitution services and negotiated fees ("Amsterdam: Legalized Prostitution," *Cultural Belle,* https://culturalbelle. wordpress.com/2013/03/28/amsterdam-legalized-prostitution/).

What did I feel? I accepted the fact that people are different, and mores evolve as society changes through culture, religious indoctrination, economic status, environmental events, and other factors.

Viking River Cruises took care of our transportation needs from the hotel to the airport and up to our flight home. My mood was somber in the plane as I would be facing the fact that my dear mother passed away three days before. I had to attend to giving her a great farewell. All I knew was that she lived a good life and was ready to go at age eighty-nine, free from any cares and pains.

Chapter 22

Our Daughter's Wedding to a Jewish Sound Engineer

Having partially addressed our financial mess, it was a feeling of joy to be at another wedding. The first wedding in my family was celebrated in the heart of Washington DC. For the second, it was in the middle of the mountains. No one could access you by phone for there was no Wi-Fi connection except at some sections by the office, and cell phone reception was spotty. We received the notice addressed to family and friends stating, "Our wedding will take place in a beautiful valley in the Catskill Mountains of New York. Due to the nature and location of our wedding, we recommend that guests stay overnight with us at the resort venue."

The rehearsal dinner was held at Zarah and Matt's home at Livingston Manor, also at the Catskills. They purchased this thirty-acre property as their weekend home, which was about a two-hour drive from Manhattan. Both of them worked with Blue Man Group at the time, Matt as chief engineer and assistant sound director, and Zarah as video production designer.

Zarah wanted to serve some Filipino dishes. We brought a twenty-eight-pound, oven-roasted suckling pig, or Philippine lechon. We ordered it from Northstar Café and Grill Catering, owned by Merlyn and John Eda, who understood that it should be special for the occasion. It was roasted to perfection, golden brown and crispy.

It came with the famous lechon sauce brand Mang Tomas. We had a great-smelling load on the back seat of the Mercedes.

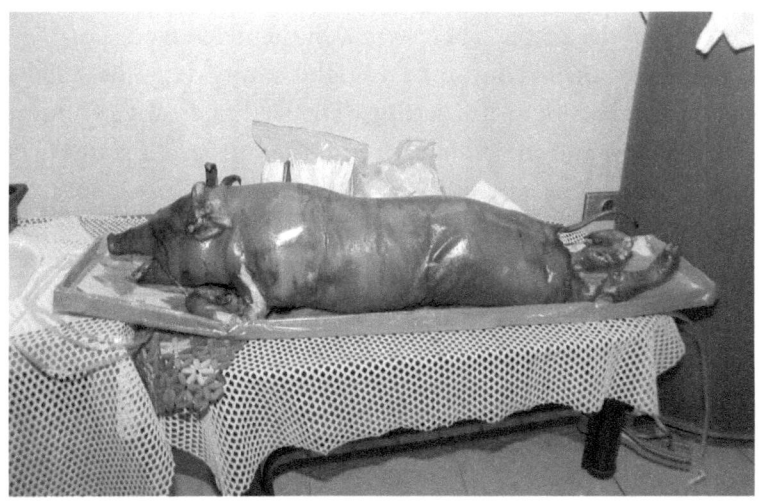

Philippine lechon from Maryland to Catskills, NY

We also served lumpia Shanghai; the generic name is egg roll. It is made of ground beef and ground pork loin with spring onions, thinly sliced baby carrots, water chestnuts, and spices rolled in thin lumpia wrapper that is fried until crunchy. Also dish served was pansit, rice noodles cooked with shredded chicken and a good cut of pork, flavored with soy sauce, spring onions, cabbage, carrots, snow peas, and spices. Matt's family are of Jewish ancestry. I was astonished that they, particularly Grandpa Harold and Grandma Jeanette, really enjoyed the lechon and all the Filipino dishes.

Our only grandchild at the time was barely walking on her own. We practiced with her so she could perform her role as a flower girl. To our surprise, Anais lived up to our expectations. Like an adult, she was ready and happy to walk alongside her aunts, Zarah's cousins Victoria and Isabelle from Henderson, Nevada, who came to assist her. A good number of Zarah's and Matt's friends and associates came. We had a great rehearsal and dinner that followed.

It was a hot summer in the Catskills in August 2014. Rain could have spoiled the event. There was a big tent reserved, but it was not needed. It turned out to be a bright, sunny day. The wedding took place at this beautiful setting. The fresh greenery of summer in the meadow and the verdant trees in the surrounding area in the Catskill Mountains were a beautiful backdrop for the upbeat and happy wedding.

Catskills wedding venue

The bride was stunning in her strapless Vera Wang gown made of fine fabric. It wrapped around her tiny waist and flowed down to her feet, extending to the back like a train. It had a very dramatic effect. Her bridal bouquet of red flowers was in perfect contrast with her bridal gown. Her entourage wore short red dresses, except for the bridesmaid, who had a long gown. They all carried bouquets of fresh white flowers that looked outstanding with their red outfits.

As for the groom, he wore a dark suit with a white shirt and a matching dark bow tie. The groomsmen wore dark suits with white shirts and red ties that complemented the ladies' red dresses and gown. The green setting of the mountain was a perfect background of these beautiful colors of white, red, blue, and black. Tony wore a white traditional Philippine formal attire called Barong Tagalog. It is made of pineapple fiber and delicately embroidered on the front and sleeves. As for me, I wore a light-gold embroidered gown with a sleeveless top.

The wedding followed a little bit of Jewish tradition. The couple stood under a canopy called chuppah while the marriage ceremony was performed. The four corners of the chuppah were held up by family members throughout the ceremony. Matt's grandfather, Harold, officiated at the wedding. It was a personalized ceremony as he spoke to the couple and told their story. Toward the end of the ceremony, Matt stepped on the glass inside a cloth bag to shatter it. Afterward, the guests shouted, "Mazel tov," meaning good luck or congratulations. It's wishing the newlyweds the best for the future and a great destiny and fortune.

At the reception, they performed a celebratory dance called the hora. Guests danced in circle while Matt and Zarah, seated on chairs, were lifted into the air while holding onto a handkerchief. This was the end of the Jewish tradition, and the regular wedding party as we knew it took over. After the wedding feast, we went to another venue for a karaoke party and more dancing. It was a very long day, but everyone seemed to have lots of energy and wanted more fun.

The following morning everyone, was invited by the groom's parents to another venue for a breakfast treat. This was an intimate gathering of close relatives and friends, who checked into rooms at the resort. After breakfast, the bride and groom hurriedly left for their honeymoon to Barcelona, Spain.

We were given enough time to prepare for this expense, so there was no need to charge our credit cards or borrow from the line of credit. We took it from our emergency funds, but it still followed our usual thinking that retirement funding of at least a million could wait. Why not? This was a once in a lifetime experience for our baby girl to have a wedding she planned with no input from me. She is a totally independent girl from Maryland but a New Yorker in so many ways.

Chapter 23
Project Repositioning for Retirement: Fourth Purchase

I was at the retina specialist's office of Dr. Robert Stephens for a regular checkup. While waiting, I had an opportunity to read magazines I no longer subscribed to, including the August 2012 *Money*. It featured an article titled, "How to Reach $1 Million: 5 Strategies to Save, Earn and Invest Your Way to Real Wealth." It was written by Carolyn Bigda, Lisa Gibbs, Elaine Pofeldt, and Donna Rosato. What a very interesting subject. Track number one was real estate. According to the authors, the key move was to expand your holdings to at least three rental properties. To produce the cumulative equity and rental earnings to reach $1 million, it was determined that it took three or more properties. It becomes easier to manage and allows cost saving measures by using a single contractor for maintenance. I also learned that Fannie Mae rules allow up 20 percent down payment for up to four properties, which includes the primary residence, and at least 25 percent for homes five to ten.

Before I was called in for my eye tests and consultation, I had already printed copy of the article courtesy of one of the staff. I was happy to read this cover story, because two months before, we had just completed our third purchase.

This information on real estate stuck with me and was critical in the closing years before retirement. It was about time to make the final move before retirement. Tony did not retire on his sixty-seventh, so I did not retire on my sixty-sixth. It was imperative for Tony to add another two years of service to have a better retirement and complete package of benefits, particularly the medical. Our retirement had to be at the same time to enjoy our travel plans. I could not do it by myself.

During this time, it was necessary to reevaluate our retirement plans and make some adjustments in our real estate portfolio. During the twenty years since our first purchase, the idea of living in a much-desired zip code stayed with me. The house that was our original choice was within that criteria, but the seller did not want to make some structural improvements. Even though the house was not as good as what we purchased, it held about 35 percent more in value due partly to the zip code.

With this in mind, I decided to check the possibility for a good buy as the interest rate was low, and home prices were stabilized. I consulted Johan, who recommended a property he thought had good potential. I handed him a check for earnest money, and we started seriously assessing the pros and cons of this property. The curb appeal was not good, it was not in move-in condition, and the location was not really good. I suggested to Johan that we look at another house we had passed by several times. It looked very impressive but might cost beyond our budget. Johan arranged for the visit. "This house has a great appeal and good vibes," Tony said. Hearing this from him was uncommon, so I decided to look seriously at the possibility of funding the purchase of our fourth property.

I couldn't believe that we, aged sixty-six and sixty-seven, were moving to a bigger and more expensive house two years before our retirement. This seemed to be unorthodox as most people our age who were retiring were downsizing. I called the move repositioning. The desire to invest in a property situated in a good, established neighborhood with a distinctive zip code was the motivating force. The house was on the market for a while, and the price was reduced. These were favorable factors for the purchase. On the day we were set to close, the purchase did not happen. No documents were presented to us. When finally received, the figures in the settlement statement did not conform to the disclosure statement, and the cost was more than what had been agreed on.

This purchase was not easy. I had not experienced this kind of stress in my past dealings. We did not know why it was made difficult. We were dictated to make improvements and repairs, and these were added as conditions of the purchase. Further, we were required to submit a proof of payment showing that these improvements, including roof replacements, were done. Our purchase was not conditional, and we had complied with the original terms of sale. So I withdrew my offer.

One good thing was we had a loan processor, Sonia Harvey of Movement Mortgage LLC, who carefully listened and intervened. She understood my concern and made corrections and recalculations without which we could have paid $10,000 more than the terms of the sale. If she hadn't, the purchase would not have been possible. The project was finally achieved.

Chapter 24
Strategic Realignment of Assets

Before the tenants of the third house moved out, Johan listed it for rent. While it was on the market for a while, it gave me an opportunity to think and analyze the prospect of this investment. Of all our properties, this one at Flora Lane had the lowest mortgage and costs, and it provided the additional retirement income that I need. But it had the least prospect of appreciation of value, even though it was in a reputable zip code, the school district and its location were not as desirable as the other three properties.

After the contract to rent with Johan expired, I transferred it to another broker and decided to sell. Brokers are clearly different. Some have a savvy style and a team that works for them. Others are solitary, like tigers. I did not follow the advice from *CNNMONEY. com*. I ended up having one, not four rental properties. We sold the Flora Lane property despite the fact that the rent income was more than double the cost of the monthly mortgage for strategic financial positioning. The property was sold ten months after the purchase of the fourth property. We were not able to take advantage of any tax-saving measures. We ended up paying more taxes on the sale. Our tax attorney made us aware that there were ways and means of savings on taxes if the sale and purchase were properly timed. This was a lesson-learning experience. I forgot an important lesson learned in BPMs:

When you earn money, they tax it.
When you spend, they tax it.
When you save, they tax it.
And when you die, they tax it.

We moved to the fourth purchased house, on Rocton Avenue, in the winter of 2016. Johan took charge of renting out our first, the Ross Road house. The house was vacant during the winter but rented out in early spring. Most of the tenants stayed at least two years, and they recommended it to their friends when they moved to another state or to their own homes. The rental income was more than enough to cover the monthly mortgage and costs, and it provided additional retirement income for us. The three rules in real estate—location, location, location—are true.

I referred back to my Wealth and Dream Notebook that I had maintained all these years. I wrote down all my goals and crazy ideas and plans on how to achieve them. It included calculations of possible results of actions and different scenarios of changes before they were executed and implemented. It was always in consultation with Tony. Should we sell Ross Road property (#1) to pay off the entire mortgage of East West Highway property (#2) or vice-versa? Should we make property 1 our primary residence and rent the Rocton Ave. property (#4)? What would be the best strategy to provide us with more cashflow while preserving our assets and accumulating more? Did we really need to? Would our retirement income and assets be sufficient to cover our long-term care needs just in case? Answers to those questions were highly dependent on our needs during our retirement years. I made a pro-forma income and expense statement, which we reviewed and reworked annually. Provisions were made for fixed monthly payables such as mortgage costs, life insurance premiums for Tony and me and for Carl and Zarah, cost-of-living expenses as budgeted, utilities and auto expenses, and for variable monthly expenses, like home improvements and maintenance, taxes, communication expenses, gifts, entertainment, travel, charity, and socialization expenses. Even if all these were factored in, we can never be sure what will happen in the future.

Without much ado, the government reduced and limited the deductibility of the real property tax. We are now paying more real property tax, and it cannot be deducted to its full amount. This was just an example of uncertainties that can cause even well-designed plans to be refigured. Consider the inflation factor and many variables. It was therefore necessary to have a cushion for the invisible and unexpected expenses in order to feel comfortable during retirement.

Here is a simple analysis in terms of percentages of our retirement income:

I: Our total retirement income is provided by:

1.	Rental income	44.0 percent
2.	Pension check and Social Security	56.0 percent
	Total	100 percent

II: Our total retirement fund is budgeted to pay for:

1.	Monthly living expenses, including gifts and entertainment	23.5 percent
2.	Mortgage payments	49.4 percent
3.	Allowance for contingencies (vacancies and credit loss; property repairs and maintenance)	08.6 percent
4.	Monthly excess, which could fund travel, emergency fund, charity, and more savings	18.5 percent
	Total	100 percent

In the beginning, I was really scared to think of retirement since our salaries would be replaced by Social Security checks and Tony's pension from the state. It was terrifying to think that our income would be reduced by as much as 57 percent. But then there was a plus factor in retirement. Payroll tax, and federal and state income taxes were eliminated or decreased, and expenses for transportation, office outfits, personal grooming, meals, drinks, and other expenses related to earning a salary were also eliminated or greatly reduced. Due to appropriate repositioning of our assets and other financial strategies, we were able to face it and deal with its challenges well.

Chapter 25
The Die Is Cast: Time Is Up

Tony and I went to the Social Security Administration and submitted our applications and the documents required. We had given notice to our employers of our intent to retire. At the time, I feared not having a million dollars in our 401k, IRA, stock market, CDs, and bank accounts would not allow us a healthy retirement. I had read and heard from the financial gurus and experts about this threshold many times, and that made me feel insecure about our retirement resources. Should we convert the real estate investments to cash and invest them in the stock market? I have very limited knowledge and exposure to investing in stocks and other marketable securities. I was fearful of going into something I did not know. Tony and I tried to learn something about it. We were invited to a business presentation about stock options trading. Options are derivatives of financial securities. It is called such because its price is linked to the price of underlying stocks, bonds, currencies, commodities, and other assets. *Investopedia* defines an option as a contract giving the buyer the right, but not the obligation, to buy (in the case of a call) or sell (in the case of a put) the underlying asset at a specific price on or before a certain date ("Options Definition," *investopedia.com*, January 1, 2022, https://www.investopedia.com/terms/o/option.asp). Options are used by people for income, speculation, and as a hedge against risk.

For a full day, we were shown the basic information and the latest technology. We were invited to attend an extensive class but should invest $20,000 up-front. You could pay by credit card or cashier's check. It was not clear what it was for. Further in the sales talk, we figured that what they were selling was the equipment, software, and lessons to fully engage in the program. We were told that by following the instructions and their system, we would be able to recoup within one month the $20,000 fee in terms of gains earned in trading options. A retired couple was there to assist in convincing the twenty or so attendees to enroll in the class. They told us they invested their retirement money in this, and they were happy they did. "Every day upon waking up this is what he does for half an hour or so," she said.

Tony gave me a sensible warning: "We will not invest in a venture that makes us as the captive consumer of their products. We will continue to pay a monthly fee for the use of their software. If the option is a derivative of an underlying asset, then we have to invest in some of these assets. It will not just involve $20,000 but could be our retirement fund, just like what the recruiter couple did."

Another thing I did was to consult a fund manager. He was referred by the attorney who worked in setting up our living trust. He told me straightforward that if we had at least half a million in investable cash, he would work with us. That was somewhat disheartening to hear, but it gave me the courage to analyze what we had at hand. Should we convert our real estate assets to cash and invest it in Wall Street? That was tough. But since we were not familiar or comfortable with intangible assets in the stock market, I did not have any second thoughts about dismissing that idea. We did not want a million-dollar retirement fund in the market.

Taking for granted that we had the funds, for it to last for twenty years, it is suggested to withdraw at most 4 percent annually to cover retirement needs. At certain times, it was also suggested to be better and withdraw 3 percent so your nest egg does not run out prior to your death. Therefore, it would be about $30,000 to $40,000 annually, or $2,500 to $3,333 per month, drawings

("How Much Retirement Income Will $1 Million Generate," July 22, 2015, https://money.cnn.com/2015/07/22/retirement/retirement-income/index.html).

Based on our monthly estimate of fixed and variable expenses, we did not need this additional income. Our combined Social Security checks and Tony's pension, 401(k), and 401(a), along with the rental income residue were more than sufficient for our retirement needs. We did not need to make any changes in our assets and investments. Our assets would continue to grow, and cash flow will improve every time there is an adjustment in rental income and value appreciation.

What is next, where do we go from here?

Chapter 26
Retirement, Travel, and Have Fun

For most of us who have dedicated thirty-five to fifty years of our lives to earning a living, retirement is the reward we are looking for. We desire not to work anymore but to enjoy the life of a retiree while still blessed with good health. I know a friend who worked very hard, saved a lot for retirement, lived frugally, never indulged in any luxury, never traveled, and hoped to do these all on her retirement. Six months in retirement, she was diagnosed with fourth-stage cancer and died without enjoying the nest egg she built. She had no family of her own, so she left a net worth to her four siblings, who each received $250,000.

A doctor-friend unfortunately married a nonearning husband who controlled their finances. She was able to free herself from this situation after she divorced him. The dream house they were building was always a work in progress and never completed. She drove a so-so car, did not travel except to attend conferences, and never spent like the millionaire she was. The divorce put her under a lot of stress. She never enjoyed her wealth for she passed away soon after her retirement, leaving everything to her two unmarried sisters.

Tony and I knew a popular figure in our community who was a playwright, composer, musician, a professional, an active volunteer, and a selfless individual. He did not live long enough to see and take pride in his children's achievements at school and in their budding careers. I had the opportunity to talk to him about life insurance, savings, and retirement. He passed away at a young age with nothing to his name. His priorities were not in the appropriate place. Some intelligent people are very knowledgeable about many things but not about the realities of life. These were instances that I was fearful of and didn't want to experience.

A year prior to retirement, Tony and I believed we were ready to face a new chapter in our lives. Included in our estimated retirement budget were items such as travel and entertainment. For us, to enjoy life is to travel and see the world. Tony and I decided to use up our paid time off prior to retirement. Otherwise, we would just lose it. So in the springtime, to sunny Spain we went.

How about a uniformed chauffeur in a well-appointed limousine service waiting at your doorstep to bring you to the airport? He was exceptionally helpful, professional, courteous, and only spoke when spoken to. Then at your destination, a similar service awaited you at the airport, holding a sign with your name on it and welcomed you warmly. You were driven peacefully in a black sedan service and settled at your designated hotel. At the conclusion of your tour, a uniformed chauffeur waited at your hotel lobby to assist you with your luggage before whisking you to the terminal for your departure. At your local airport, you are met and driven straight to your home. All these amenities were arranged by Collette Tours.

Spain, as I stated previously, was the colonial power that occupied the Philippines for around 333 years. Unlike other colonies of Spain, Spanish is not the country's language. Most Filipinos have Spanish last names and are predominantly Catholics. Filipinos speak and understand English, though the US colonization of the Philippines lasted only forty-eight years. My interest in Spain was based not only due to my familiarity and understanding of its history, art, culture, food, and language but the reputation that it is a beautiful country with mountain ranges, plains, beaches, and lakes, and a welcoming, happy people.

The Spain tour with Collette enabled us to visit the cities of Madrid, Toledo, Cordoba, Seville, Granada, Valencia, Barcelona, and Montserrat. We started the tour in Madrid with a welcome dinner at La Galette 2, an exquisite restaurant. Used predominantly in Mediterranean cuisine are olive oil as cooking agent or dressing and fresh herbs such as oregano, saffron, basil, thyme, rosemary, cilantro, fennel, parsley, and many more flavorful and aromatic herbs. Beef is used sparingly. More popular are pork, goat, sheep, chicken, and some wild games. Preponderant use of seafood is due to its proximity to the Mediterranean Sea. Fresh vegetables are in abundance in Spain, thus their appearance in all forms of cooking.

Toledo is set on a hill high above the Tajo River (Spanish for Tagus River). Even from afar and going into the city, it is as impressive as it is from within. It is an ancient city, a UNESCO site, and until 1560, the capital of Spain ("Was Toledo once the Capital of Spain?" *Colors*, NewYork.com, https://colors-newyork. com/was-toledo-once-the-capital-of-spain/).

The drive from Madrid, its present capital, was only an hour. The various cultures of Christians, Muslims, and the Jewish were reflected in its history. We visited and enjoyed the architectural marvels of the Primate Cathedral of Saint Mary of Toledo (Toledo Cathedral), a Catholic church. Its Jewish heritage was represented therein by a thirteenth-century synagogue. Inside the Church of Santo Tome, you can find El Greco's masterpiece, *The Burial of Count Orgaz* (Church of Santo Tomé [Toledo] in Toledo | spain.info in, https:// www.spain.info/en/places-of-interest/church-santo-tome-toledo/).

Cordoba is another Moorish city that is a UNESCO site. The main architectural marvel is the Mosque Cathedral of Cordoba, also called the Cathedral of Our Lady of the Assumption. Due to its status as a former Islamic mosque, it is also known as the Great Mosque of Cordoba, or the Mezquita. The building has a total dimension of approximately 24,000 square meters, or 258,000 square feet. There are as many as 856 esthetic columns made of marble, granite, jasper, and other fine materials. The Mezquita is most notable for its red and white giant arches ("Mezquita Mosque

and Cathedral—CORDOBA 24," https://www.cordoba24.info/
english/html/mezquita.html).

This is one of the most intriguing interior structures I have seen
so far. We visited the Jewish quarter of Cordoba, where the Jews
lived during the Muslim rule. During this period, the Jews were
generally accepted in the society, and Jewish religious, cultural, and
economic life flourished.

In Seville you'll find the world's largest Gothic cathedral, the
Holy Church Seville Cathedral. It stands in an area of approximately
23,500 square meters, or 252,952 square feet. This impressive
cathedral is situated in Santa Cruz, Seville's tourist center. Also
marvelous is Giralda Tower, standing at 96 meters or 315 feet from
the ground to its weather vane (*Brochure of the Holy Church Seville
Cathedral Plan of the Cultural Visit*, www. Catedralsevilla.es).

Another important landmark we visited was the Real Alcazar
de Sevilla. It is a beautiful palace showcasing Moorish and Spanish
Christian architecture, landscapes, ponds, fountains, sculptures, and
various species of plants and flowers in the gardens (*Brochure of Real
Alcazar Sevilla*, www.patronato-alcazarsevilla.es).

We had a delicious lunch in the former Jewish quarter before
proceeding to Maria Luisa Park and the Plaza de España aboard a
horse-drawn carriage passing along the main thoroughfares of Seville.
Plaza de Espana is a square with a floor area of 45,932 square meters
or 494,408 square feet. It was built in 1928 for the Ibero-American
Exposition of 1929. The semicircle landmark is one of the most
interesting structures in Sevilla ("Plaza de España, Seville." *Wikipedia*,
https://en.wikipedia.org/wiki/Plaza_de_Espa%C3%B1a,_Seville).

Seville is one of the first southern cities of Spain where the flamenco
dance originated. We went to one of the top pure flamenco venues,
El Palacio Andaluz. The flamenco is an art form of dancing, singing,
and guitar playing. It is characterized by clapping, fast footwork, and
storytelling through song and dance with colorful costumes, canes,
shawls, fans, and castanets. The performance was superb, and the music

was uplifting and the tempo fast and exciting. We enjoyed a beautiful evening of music and dance ("Top 10 Flamenco Shows in Seville," *Welcome to Seville*, https://welcometoseville.com/flamenco-in-seville/).

We next visited Granada. It is the capital city and also the name of the province in the Andalusian region in the southeastern part of Spain. Famous places to visit in Granada are the Alhambra and Generalife (pronounced as Ge-ne-ra-lee-fee), which means, "garden of the architect." The Alhambra, a UNESCO site, is a palace built chiefly between 1238 and 1358 in the reign of Ibn al-Ahmar and his successors. It was converted to a royal court of Catholic monarchs Ferdinand and Isabella in 1492.

We visited the Alcazaba, or citadel, the military area of the huge complex of Alhambra. We also visited the Nasrid Palaces, composed of Mexuar Palace, the semipublic part of the palace used for administration of justice and for matters of the state; Comares Palace, the official residence of the king; and the Palace of the Lions, the residence of the ruler's wives, concubines, and female servants. There was a fountain supported by twelve white-marble lions. Thus, it called the Fountain of the Lions. In this section was the Court of the Myrtles, which was dominated by the central pond and made gorgeous by the contrast of colors of the bright-green myrtle bushes and the white marble of the patio.

One section of the Alhambra that I found astonishing was Generalife. It included the Generalife Palace, which was the recreation area of the kings of Granada, the lower gardens, and the upper gardens. Our guide told us to imagine people living in the Alhambra, the orchards, gardens, and animals that needed water. How was water supplied in the palaces and the land? The water was drawn from the Darro River, which was 3.8 miles away, and there was a water distribution system via surface canals and tunnels. There were also conduits, water tanks, and a complex water system, all designed and created during the thirteenth century.

The architecture, water system, expanse of the Alhambra's

structures, the beautiful arches, waterfalls, foliage, trees, the gardens and courtyards in the palaces, were just as mesmerizing and amazing. Alhambra is one of the places that I would love to visit again for its richness in history and the marvelous architecture and artistic designs ("Alhambra," *HISTORY*, March 12, 2018, https://www. history.com/topics/landmarks/alhambra).

Every place we go elicited from us an enormous amount of interest. Enroute to Valencia, we passed the Sierra Nevada Mountain range on the west and the coastline of the Mediterranean on the east. In the Andalusia region, the landscape is that of rolling hills with olive and almond groves dotting alongside the highway. Spain is reportedly the leading producer and exporter of olive oil, outranking Italy ("Olive Oil Production by Country," *WorldAtlas*, https://www. worldatlas.com/articles/olive-oil-production-by-country.html).

Valencia is on the Mediterranean coast, and as I mentioned earlier, it was once a capital of Spain and is rich in history and modern culture. It has the busiest container port in Europe. We joined a walking tour of Valencia with a very energetic local tour guide. There is a historic, or old, Valencia and the new Valencia. We saw the fourteenth-century Serranos Tower and fifteenth-century Quart Towers. Both towers were part of the city's walls. The Quart Towers were used as a prison for centuries ("Valencia, Spain— Quart and Serranos Towers," https://veryvalencia.com/things-to-do/ attractions/valencia-old-town/82-quart-and-serranos-towers).

Next was a walk toward Valencia's Central Market, one of the largest in Europe, with 8,000 square meters, or 86,111 square feet. Its architecture was again another marvel. It looks like a cathedral with a dome and slopes that provide plenty of natural light. There is beautiful use of colorful ceramic tiles, iron, glass, bricks, and stones. It was exciting to shop for souvenirs and gifts for friends in the United States. We discovered many interesting things, like saffron, olives, hams, cheeses, wines, nuts, spices and herbs, fresh produce, meats, and everything you need. We also found cooked foods, and it was all under one roof ("Central Market in Valencia" | spain.info in English, https://www.spain.info/en/places-of-interest/mercado-central-valencia/).

Our guide was very proud to take us to her home city of Valencia, where paella was first made. There was a demonstration of paella making using a pan that was so large it contained more than enough to feed about eighty of us.

Paella demonstration in Valencia

The original recipe used rabbit meat, but for us, it was chicken, "History and Origins of Paella—Iberica Spanish Food," https://www.ibericafood.com/blog/history-and-origins-of-paella-b33.html). I know rabbit meat tastes like chicken as I have tasted it, not knowing it was rabbit, at a restaurant in McLean, Virginia. That was years ago. Rabbit is not part of our customary source of protein.

To make the trip to this remote part of Valencia more interesting, there was a visit to a traditional fisherman's home, called a *barraca*, and a boat ride on the canals surrounding the rice fields on our way back. When we reached the bank on the other side, the motor coach was waiting to take us back to our hotel.

We had free time in the afternoon, the we didn't want to miss the City of Arts and Sciences. This modern facility was constructed on the former bed of Turia River, which was drained and rerouted after catastrophic flooding in 1957. The picturesque complex is made up of several buildings and structures such as the Hemisferic, designed to resemble like a giant eye. The complex has an IMAX cinema, planetarium, and laserium. The science museum is designed to look like the skeleton of a whale. The Umbracle, an open structure envelops a landscape walk with plant species indigenous to Valencia. It also serves as an outdoor art gallery, with sculptures surrounded by various plants that change colors during each season, and a car park. Oceanografic is an open-air oceanographic park. With 110,000 square meters, or 1,184,030 square feet, and 42 million liters or, 11,095,219 US gallons, it was easy to see how it earned the reputation of being the largest oceanographic aquarium in Europe. It was built in the shape of a water lily pad. The Palau de les Arts Reina Sofia is an opera house and performing arts center. Agora is the multifunctional covered space with an open ground plan where concerts and sporting events are held.

Two modern bridges are situated in the Arts and Science Complex. Both cross the dry Turia riverbed. Montolivet Bridge is a concrete road bridge, and the more impressive Assut de l'Or Bridge, is a white cable-stayed bridge sustained by a curved pylon with back-stayed counterweights. The pylon of the bridge, at 125 meters high, is the highest point in Valencia. What a feeling to have walked several times on this beautiful and impressive bridge overlooking the Arts and Science Complex, ("Assut de l'Or Bridge," *Wikipedia*, https://en.wikipedia.org/wiki/Assut_de_l%27Or_Bridge).

We were able to appreciate the expanse of the complex while observing many people enjoying the promenades and hearing the loud cheering of people as they watched a live musical show. Time did not allow us the chance to attend any ongoing events at the complex. That could be a reason to visit this wonderful place again ("City of Arts and Sciences," *Wikipedia*, https://en.wikipedia.org/wiki/City_of_Arts_and_Sciences).

Barcelona here we come. It is considered as one of Europe's most beautiful and exciting cities. What I loved about Barcelona was the vibrancy of the people, pedestrian-friendly boulevards, transportation accessibility, parks with greenery and flowers, entertainment, walkable points of interest, food, and the beautiful architecture of buildings, monuments, and churches.

Collette booked us at the Hotel Colon in Avenida Cathedral. We took advantage of our free time by exploring the famous La Rambla, which was walking distance from the hotel. This boulevard is lined with mature trees and dotted with colorful flower and vegetable stalls. There were many performing human statues. You can also find a Joan Miro mosaic, music venues, and many shops and restaurants around the area. Close by was the Picasso Museum, and across from the hotel was the Basilica Santa Maria del Mar.

On our second day in Barcelona, the local tour guide took us for a drive of Parc de Montjuic. We passed a broad, shallow hill with the highest point at 606 feet. Montjuic is strategically located overlooking the Mediterranean and alongside the Llobregat River. Views of Barcelona from outside the Palau Nacional were spectacular and of astonishingly indescribable beauty. Montjuic Parc hosted the 1929 International Exposition, a World's Fair. Located on this hill are the Olympic Stadium and Miramar Terminal of the Port Vell Aerial tramway, among others.

The Palau Nacional houses the Museu Nacional d'Art de Catalunya that extensively showcases Catalan painting and sculpture ("Montjuïc," *Wikipedia*, https://en.wikipedia.org/wiki/Montju%C3%AFc).

Magic Fountain of Montjuic is a must-see attraction. It is a fountain of colorful lights in motion and with music. Seven hundred gallons of water are sprayed through 3,620 jets, making it a magical sight to behold ("Magic Fountain of Montjuïc," *Wikipedia*, https://en.wikipedia.org/wiki/Magic_Fountain_of_Montju%C3%AFc).

Antoni Gaudi's UNESCO World Heritage sites, including La

Sagrada Familia and Parc Guell were the main attractions, and our knowledgeable local guide spent much time explaining them. She and probably most of the guides in Barcelona, Catalan, and Spain have mastered these facts about Antoni Gaudi's architectural style, which is called Modernisme, or Art Nouveau. Basilica de la Sagrada Familia is his most famous work. It is a Roman Catholic minor basilica of Gothic and Art Nouveau styles. It is still unfinished, though construction started in 1882. Of its original design of eighteen monumental spires, only eight have been built. The construction was funded from private donations.

Parc Guell is a public park with gardens and architectural structures designed by Gaudi and his collaborators. The owner of the property, Eusebi Guell, originally intended it to be just a residential estate for the wealthy families. Gaudi's design incorporated his technical expertise and mastery of forms and materials. He is known for trencadis, a decorative system consisting of cladding surfaces with small pieces of broken tiles, glass, glazed china, shells, pottery, and other small materials. Some of were often taken from demolition materials and disused objects. Gaudi completely emerged himself in his job, and Guell Park reflects his artistic work full of symbolic objects.

The residential purpose was abandoned, and it has been a public park since 1926. Only two houses were built—the white Casa Trias and a pink showhouse for the estate. The latter was Gaudi's home until shortly before his death in 1926. It is now the Gaudi House Museum. The combination of architecture and nature made it an exceptional marvelous art ("The 7 UNESCO World Heritage Sites By Gaudi You Can't Miss," January 25, 2017, https://bunkersbarcelona.com/the-7-unesco-world-heritage-sites-by-gaudi/.

Gaudi set out to provide practical solutions, such as planning for viaducts and paths for people on foot, demarcating plots and setting up water-collection systems, though at the same time the results went far beyond that, with the aspiration of achieving a total work of art and severing the dividing lines between nature, or creation, and art understood as human production. (Museu D'Historia de Barcelona)

We viewed the Columbus Monument (Mirador de Colon), built in honor of the explorer of the New World, who was commissioned by the Spanish monarchs Ferdinand and Isabella. We went to see other famous buildings built by the famous Spanish architect Antoni Gaudi, including the Batllo House and the Casa Mila Building.

I believe these creations of Antoni Gaudi are famous because of their extraordinary and uncommon designs, use of symbolism through nature and the spiritual, use of unusual materials and processes, and functionality. They are truly unique and intriguing structural arts.

Our trip arranged by Collette ended with a farewell dinner. But this was not the end of our visit in Spain. Tony and I flew from Barcelona back to the Andalusian region to visit one of Tony's high school classmates, who lives with her husband in El Romeral, Granada. We spent four days with Ofelia and Michael at their villa.

This was another perspective of life in Spain. They were both retired and expats from England. They live far from the city, and I didn't see any neighbors around, although someone came to help out in the yard and with other chores.

They drove us to some interesting places. Along the way, we saw many groves of olives and almonds. We walked on the plank on the side of the mountain, below which was the gushing water of the river. We enjoyed the verdant scenery in Parque Natural Sierra de Castril. We went to Negratin Reservoir, which was by a very clear lake that reflected the sky without any current or ripple. In Baza, we shopped at a factory that made authentic Spanish smoked legs of ham and another that specializes in sausages. We went to a bakery that makes the freshest bread to one that manufactures only cheeses. And we went to a store that sells olives, wines, and olive oil. We went to a local market where all kinds of produce and products—from fruits, vegetables, and meat to clothes, plants, cooked meals—and just about any other things you might need were sold. I bought a nice, embroidered, dainty, pastel-colored blouse for me, and for Tony, denim shorts that fit him well. The prices were a total bargain.

Along the highway on our way to Baza, they pointed out the cave houses of Galera. There were so many of them. This was strange to me. I can't believe there are people still living in caves in the twenty-first century. There were many cave-house communities in the area, but Guadix, southwest of Baza, has the largest number of underground dwellings in all Europe. There were cave churches, restaurants, hotels, and rentals. The cave homes had facilities just like surface homes. Some had swimming pools and were situated on one-acre lots with over five thousand square feet of living space. Cave dwellers, called troglodytes, have been living in caves for hundreds of years ("Guadix Cave Houses in Spain Revive Troglodyte Living," June 13, 2017, https://www.tourismontheedge.com/guadix-cave-houses/).

Cave houses in Galera, Spain

Ofelia and Michael are avid collectors of antiquities. I enjoyed the large, valuable collection of porcelain, jars, paintings, furniture, plates, vases, religious icons, and many collectibles spread all over their home.

It was also time to catch up on our lives prior to retirement and many other things about careers and journeys in our lives. The idea of holding a reunion of Tony and Ofelia's high school classmates in the United States was conceptualized during this visit.

This Spanish sojourn of fourteen days greatly motivated us in our desire to make the most of our retirement years. Another escapade was planned for a thirty-seven-day tour of the Iberian Peninsula the following year.

Chapter 27

Mission Accomplished: In the Year We Never Prepared for, We Were Prepared

We were amid the coronavirus-19, or COVID-19, pandemic. In a press release dated January 21, 2020, the Centers for Disease Control and Prevention (CDC) confirmed the first case of 2019 Novel Coronavirus (2019-nCoV) in the state of Washington. The patient had returned from Wuhan, China, where an outbreak of pneumonia caused by this coronavirus had been ongoing since December 2019. In March 2020, the World Health Organization declared COVID-19 a global pandemic. A pandemic is an outbreak of a highly contagious virus that has spread over several countries or continents, usually affecting a large number of people and causing high degree of mortality ("COVID-19 Pandemic," *Wikipedia,* https://en.wikipedia.org/wiki/COVID-19_pandemic).

For our family, giving birth to an infant in a hospital in Manhattan was a dangerous option. Zarah and Matt moved out of the city for their safety from the rapidly spreading coronavirus. Their second child was born in May 2020, at their home at the Catskills in Upstate New York. They were assisted by a midwife with prearranged services of a doctor at a hospital in case of emergency.

In July, we all decided to visit baby Uma, our fourth grandchild and newest addition to the family. Carl and his family came from Columbus, Ohio, and Tony and I drove up from Chevy Chase, Maryland. All of us, including our hosts, slept in their own tents, observed physical distancing, wore face masks and shields, and maintained handwashing and sanitizing protocols and a bathroom schedule.

Only Matt and Zarah went inside their house for food preparation and supplies. We each had assigned places to sit and eat. Our grandchildren—Anais, seven; Felix, four; and Raphael, three—easily followed the safety rules, and no one complained. They were excited to play together and performed their dance routine as choreographed by Anais. Felix proudly led his cousins in exploring the forest and identifying some of the edible plants and herbal and medicinal trees he learned from his parents.

Space Acres tents during Covid-19 Pandemic

This idea for this memoir came during this family get-together at Zarah and Matt's Space Acres. Zarah was amazed how we maneuvered our way through the past thirty years. Tony remembered that years before retirement was even on our minds, Carl had said, "Dad, Mom, please make sure that you have enough funds for your retirement." The statement was a good reminder for us at that time. Carl knew that in the Philippines, the culture was entirely different. Children took care of their elderly parents in return for and appreciation of the sacrifices they made on their behalf by sending them to college and spending all their resources just to get through it. Discussion of the family living trust was timely. We were thankful that despite bumps and stops, our strategies worked, and our goals were accomplished at the most opportune time. The retirement pro-forma budget we prepared would meet our needs and provide a sense of security for the coming years. Our mission to provide our children with a good education so they could become self-sufficient and provide and care for their own families is done. We accomplished our desire to live debt-free and pay cash for our expenses and purchases, with the exception of good mortgage debts on the properties. Our travel plans were in order, and we hope to enjoy them while we have the energy and good health to do so. As of now, our fourth purchase is a good home for us. As to our legacy, we can very well say that we will leave behind to our children a strong sense of responsibility and desire to be good parents to their young.

Tony and I do not believe in giving them an advance inheritance. They have to test their capabilities to make good and to do their best to provide for their families and to accumulate on their own. They should leave their marks in ways best suited for them.

We hope to leave this place better than we have found it.